AF255993

Linking Mine Action and SSR through Human Security

Ursign Hofmann, Gianluca Maspoli,
Åsa Massleberg and Pascal Rapillard

Published by
Ubiquity Press Ltd.
6 Osborn Street, Unit 2N
London E1 6TD

First published 2016
Transferred to Ubiquity Press 2018

Editors: Heiner Hänggi & Albrecht Schnabel
Associate editor: Fairlie Chappuis
Editorial assistance: Kathrin Reed
Copy editor: Cherry Ekins

DOI: https://doi.org/10.5334/bbz

This book was originally published by the Geneva Centre for the Democratic Control of Armed Forces (DCAF), an international foundation whose mission is to assist the international community in pursuing good governance and reform of the security sector. The title transferred to Ubiquity Press when the series moved to an open access platform. The full text of this book was peer reviewed according to the original publisher's policy at the time. The original ISBN for this title was 978-92-9222-413-4.

SSR Papers is a flagship DCAF publication series intended to contribute innovative thinking on important themes and approaches relating to security sector reform (SSR) in the broader context of security sector governance (SSG). Papers provide original and provocative analysis on topics that are directly linked to the challenges of a governance-driven security sector reform agenda. SSR Papers are intended for researchers, policy-makers and practitioners involved in this field.

The views expressed are those of the author(s) alone and do not in any way reflect the views of the institutions referred to or represented within this paper.

Suggested citation:
Hofmann, U., Maspoli, G., Massleberg, Å. and Rapillard, P. 2018. *Linking Mine Action and SSR through Human Security*. London: Ubiquity Press. DOI: https://doi.org/10.5334/bbz. License: CC-BY 4.0

Contents

Introduction*

Security sector reform (SSR) and mine action occur in many different settings ranging from war-torn to post-conflict and developed countries. However, both fields of activity are most commonly implemented in post-conflict contexts. The United Nations (UN) Capstone Doctrine testifies to this view by listing SSR and mine action among the "critical peacebuilding activities",[1] alongside disarmament, demobilization and reintegration (DDR), protection and promotion of human rights, electoral assistance and support to state authority. Mindful of this fact and the window of opportunities resulting from it, the present research focuses on post-conflict peacebuilding contexts.

Despite their relevance in post-conflict peacebuilding, SSR and mine action seem to belong to separate communities of practice and the linkages between the two fields remain weak. This paper aims to address this disconnection by seeking to answer the following research questions.

- What are the conceptual linkages between SSR and mine action?
- To what extent and how are these conceptual linkages operationalized on the ground?
- How could the interaction between SSR and mine action be more effectively operationalized?

---

* The authors express their gratitude to Jakob Donatz for his assistance and support in the initial phases of writing this paper.

The paper posits that SSR and mine action have a strong common conceptual basis, which draws from a shared understanding of security. They both contribute to a concept of security that is not limited to the level of the state, but takes into account security threats and needs at societal and individual levels. This common basis provides opportunities for synergies between SSR and mine action, by which we understand the possibility of achieving greater impact through improved interaction rather than actions implemented in silos.[2]

However, empirical evidence demonstrates that linkages and interactions between SSR and mine action remain limited and underexplored. The respective programmes have a tendency to be implemented in distinct clusters, without much interaction. This paper argues that stronger linkages between SSR and mine action would be beneficial for both domains, and that the concept of human security provides a comprehensive framework which can bridge the differences and open broader opportunities for cooperation.

The first section of the paper aims to demonstrate that SSR and mine action reflect a similar conceptualization of security – human security. The second section shows how this similarity is translated into a common theoretical approach in establishing and implementing programmes. The third section is empirical and explores how SSR and mine action interact at operational level, both within and beyond UN peacekeeping/peacebuilding missions. The conclusion sums up the findings and depicts how the concept of human security may help in strengthening synergies between SSR and mine action.

Conceptualization of Security: A Broadened Perspective

This section demonstrates that SSR and mine action contribute to the same concept of security, namely human security, and that the emergence of this concept influenced the evolution of both SSR and mine action towards a broadening of their respective fields of activity. The section also addresses the impact of this broadened perspective on security in post-conflict peacekeeping and peacebuilding, and thereby how SSR and mine action have become essential programmes in such contexts. It lays the conceptual foundation based on which the paper scrutinizes the existing and potential interaction between SSR and mine action.

Human security as a conceptual framework: Objectives and principles

Security has traditionally been understood as a matter of survival or self-preservation of the state, with defence issues such as border control and military posture at the forefront. In the post-Cold War era, civil wars increasingly emerged as the most common form of armed conflict instead of interstate wars, affecting more and more civilian populations. As a result, the traditional concept of security has widened and deepened, based on the recognition that insecurity might stem not only from military threats but also from environmental, societal, political and economic threats.[3]

This broader concept of security has led to the understanding that individuals and communities should be the core security concern, and that the security sector should provide protection from both external and internal threats without becoming a threat itself.[4] In the words of former Canadian foreign minister, Lloyd Axworthy, "it has become clear that individual security is not necessarily the product of national security [and it requires] a shift in focus, from ensuring peace across State borders to building peace within States".[5] Logically, this leads to the assumption that the security of the state and the security of its people are interdependent, and the state is not secure when its population is not secure.[6]

Human security also provides an alternative perspective on state sovereignty which, in its traditional sense, relies upon the government's control over a territory, the independence of the state and its recognition by other states. While the human security approach of course does not remove state sovereignty, it reverses equation: The state is obliged to serve and support its people, from whom it draws, in theory, its legitimacy.[7]

The concept of human security was popularised by the 1994 UN Development Programme (UNDP) *Human Development Report*,[8] which raised the importance of threats to human rights, security and development in the efforts to fight poverty and improve livelihoods. The Report noted that human security has always been defined as freedom from fear and freedom from want.[9] Political, economic, societal and environmental threats began to be addressed as threats to security,[10] and led to the acknowledgement that the lack of security of people—and not only states—was a major impediment to poverty reduction and development.[11]

It is not the purpose of this paper to discuss in depth the debate among scholars, practitioners and politicians on the concept of human security. However, it is worth briefly indicating that the understanding of what human security means and what it encompasses has not been unchallenged. In particular, some critics view an approach of "freedom from fear and freedom from want" as too broad, both for theoretical and policy-oriented reasons.[12] Firstly, by considering more harms as security threats, it becomes more difficult to study the relations and causalities between them. Secondly, the broad definition can also be problematic for its use at policy level.[13] This school of thinking suggests a narrower interpretation that focuses on human security as freedom from fear, meaning the threat or use of physical violence.

It was only in 2012 that the international community agreed on a definition of human security, enshrined in UN Resolution 66/290. This definition considers human security as an approach aimed at "identifying and addressing widespread and cross-cutting challenges to the survival, livelihood and dignity of [member states'] people", entailing among others the "the right of people to live in freedom and dignity, free from poverty and despair" and entitling them "to freedom from fear and freedom from want, with an equal opportunity to enjoy all their rights and fully develop their human potential".[14] The backbone of this approach is that security is people-centred, comprehensive, context-specific, prevention-oriented and nationally owned. States bear the primary responsibility for ensuring the survival, livelihoods and dignity of their citizens.

In the same resolution, the interlinkages between peace, development and human rights are clearly articulated. It is argued that SSR and mine action share many of the building blocks, goals and approaches of human security. Some stakeholders even perceive the global movement to ban anti-personnel landmines in the 1990s, with its emphasis on the humanitarian impact rather than the national security aspects of their use, as a starting point for the human security approach.[15] In the following subsections the evolution of SSR, mine action and UN peacekeeping/building operations is analysed within this broadened and more holistic understanding of security.

Security sector reform: Towards comprehensive security and good governance

The concept of SSR emerged with the end of the Cold War and has contributed to overcoming the traditional definition of security as a field limited exclusively to the military dimensions of state defence. In particular, as shown in Figure 1, SSR has produced a double broadening of the concept of security.[16] Firstly, SSR broadens the range of actors typically associated with security by integrating other dimensions of state security provision besides the military. Secondly, SSR broadens our understanding of security by moving beyond the state as the only beneficiary of security to account for the security of individuals and social groups.

Figure 1: Holistic nature of SSR[17]

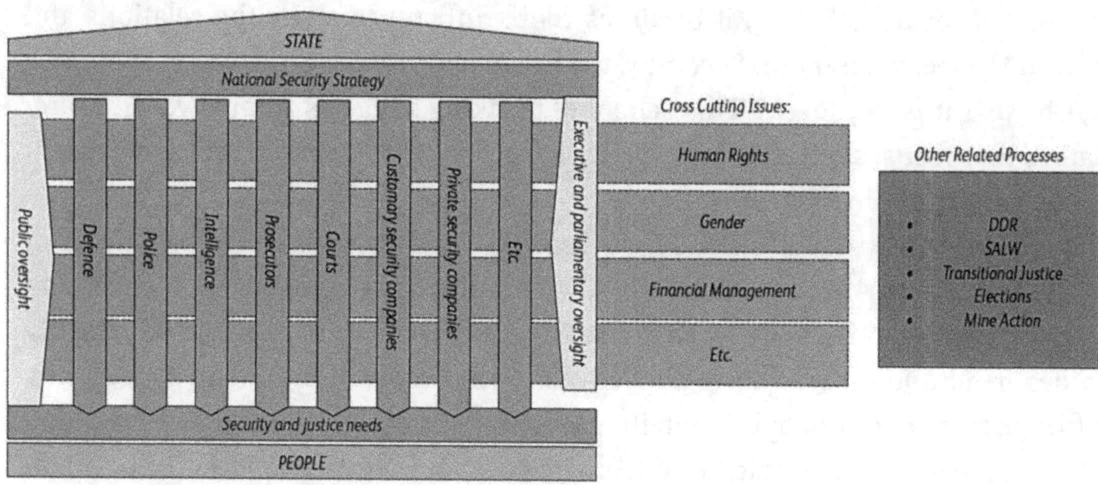

Like the concept of human security, SSR thus reflects the need to address security concerns in a comprehensive manner. However, SSR does not consist only of this broader view, but also entails a specific focus on the management and oversight of the agencies and institutions responsible for delivering security. In other words, at the core of SSR there is not only the question of effective delivery of security but also a concern for ensuring that such delivery respects democratic principles, the rule of law and human rights.[18] Ultimately, effectiveness and accountability are not separable, and both are essential for determining the nature and content of the reforms that are needed to achieve security for the state and its people.

SSR has been recognized by many major international bodies and states as a crucial prerequisite for security, peace and development. Despite this, no generally accepted definition of SSR has yet been proposed, but it is frequently acknowledged that there is some convergence around the definitions put forward by the Development Assistance Committee of the Organization for Economic Co-operation and Development (OECD-DAC) and the UN.

In its 2005 guidelines on *Security Sector Reform and Governance*, the OECD-DAC describes SSR as seeking "to increase partner countries' ability to meet the range of security needs within their societies in a manner consistent with democratic norms and sound governance principles, including transparency and the rule of law".[19] In the UN context, SSR has been defined as "a process of assessment, review and implementation as well as monitoring and evaluation led by national authorities that has as its goal the enhancement of effective and accountable security for the State and its peoples without discrimination and with full respect for human rights and the rule of law".[20] Although not identical, both these definitions have been interpreted as essentially agreeing on three core features of SSR.

First, SSR must be a locally owned process, meaning that "the reform of security policies, institutions and activities in a given country must be designed, managed and implemented by local actors rather than external actors".[21] While it is true that what can and cannot be achieved by SSR efforts is often greatly dependent on local power relations and political will, it is also important to emphasize that local ownership is not synonymous with government ownership.[22] Rather, it implies a people-centred approach that considers the needs of all stakeholders, particularly those in the most vulnerable and disenfranchised groups.

Second, the two main objectives of the reform process are enhanced effectiveness and accountability of the security sector. The former refers to the capability of the security sector to meet the security and justice needs of a country's population adequately and ensure the overall well-being of the state and its citizens. Accountability denotes the manner in which security is provided. It entails the existence of checks and balances to safeguard against power abuses and guarantee that all actors in the security sector provide their services in accordance with the law. The normative assumptions in this context usually promote democratic and civilian oversight of the security sector, transparency and the protection of human rights as indispensable elements of sustainable accountability.[23]

A final feature on which most definitions agree is that SSR employs a holistic approach to reflect the system-wide interconnectedness of security issues. It makes little sense, for example, to improve the operability of the law enforcement sector if at the same time mechanisms to interpret the law fail to meet even a minimum standard of accountability and legitimacy. In accordance with a holistic approach, reform efforts are therefore not limited to statutory security providers (the armed forces, police, intelligence services, etc.), but also engage with security management and oversight bodies (parliament and its relevant legislative committees, the government, including ministries of defence, etc.); justice and rule of law institutions (justice ministries, prisons, the judiciary, human rights commissions and ombuds offices, etc.); non-statutory security forces (liberation armies, guerrilla armies, private military and security companies, political party militias, etc.); and civil society groups (the media, research institutions, religious bodies, non-governmental organizations (NGOs) and community groups, etc.).[24] However, this does not mean that SSR should always encompass reforms of all the components of the security sector. What is essential is to grasp that any SSR programme, even a narrow one, requires a comprehensive understanding of the security sector.[25] Disregarding the holistic nature of any SSR process would lead to the "fatal mistake" of believing that effectiveness alone could "trigger commitment to good governance and a more comprehensive SSR approach".[26]

From these three core features, it is important to emphasize three characteristics of SSR that become important when we look at its linkages with mine action. First, SSR is essentially a political process because it touches on capacities and functions related to the state's monopoly of the legitimate use of force.[27] In fact, regardless of the specificities of the implementation context, SSR affects not only capacities in delivering security but also the control over and oversight of security providers, and consequently it impacts the balance of power between the state and the society and among political actors. The political nature of SSR explains why it is particularly sensitive in post-conflict contexts, where the state is weak and other actors have significant power and influence on politics. In such contexts, the challenge for SSR is to overcome resistance and manipulation aiming at preserving or increasing control over the security services.[28]

Second, SSR is affected by the context, and "no one-size-fits-all"[29] approach works. This characteristic is related to the political nature of SSR, and its implementation demands a profound understanding of local political actors and dynamics.

Third, SSR needs to consider a number of cross-cutting issues, like human rights, gender and financial management, as well as related processes, including DDR, small arms and light weapons (SALW) control, transitional justice and mine action.[30] This need is the direct consequence of a broadened understanding of security, and more specifically of the SSR focus on good governance and people's security. In operational terms, this means that SSR requires a wide range of skills and the adoption of a multidisciplinary approach – SSR measures are unlikely to succeed if implemented in isolation from other peacebuilding, post-conflict reconstruction and development programmes.

These three characteristics show that the concept of SSR brings a significant contribution to the broadening of the concept of security and is consistent with the human security perspective. Thus human security provides a basis for identifying common features with mine action and potential synergies. Having reviewed the evolution of SSR in this subsection, we next analyse the evolution of mine action to illustrate how it has also moved towards a more holistic response.

Mine action: From humanitarian demining to explosive hazard management

The UN International Mine Action Standards (IMAS) – a set of sector-wide standards providing guidance, establishing principles and defining requirements designed to improve safety, efficiency and effectiveness – define mine action as "activities which aim to reduce the social, economic and environmental impact of mines and ERW [explosive remnants of war] including unexploded sub-munitions".[31] Consequently, mine action is not only about clearing land, but equally about people and societies at large and how they are affected[32] by landmines[33] and ERW,[34] with the ultimate goal of reducing the risks to a level "where people can live safely; in which economic, social and health development can occur free from the constraints imposed by landmine and ERW contamination; and in which the victims' needs can be addressed".[35] Nowadays, mine action is commonly understood to comprise five complementary groups of activities or "pillars":

- mine/ERW risk education (MRE);
- demining, i.e. mine/ERW survey, mapping, marking and clearance;
- victim assistance, including rehabilitation and reintegration;
- stockpile destruction;
- advocacy against the use of anti-personnel mines and cluster munitions.[36]

The origins of mine action can be traced back to 1988, when for the first time the UN appealed for funds in a humanitarian response to the problems caused by landmines in Afghanistan. The appeal related to "humanitarian demining", a new term which was understood to mean removal of emplaced mines and also information and education activities to prevent injuries. The term "humanitarian demining" was used to denote mine clearance for humanitarian purposes and distinguish it clearly from the military activity of "breaching", which cleared paths through minefields to attain military mission objectives during combat operations.

The creation of the world's first international humanitarian mine clearance NGOs in the late 1980s further accelerated the shift from military to humanitarian demining. Even more so, the growing importance of commercial demining companies following the clean-up of Kuwait after the Gulf War in 1991 further contributed to the affirmation of mine action as a professional civilian activity.[37] Today around 40 states and territories have established some form of mine action programme, while in some other states and territories mine action activities are overseen by the UN.

Over time, the concept and scope of mine action have widened incrementally. In its earliest days, it focused on landmines exclusively. It soon became clear that other forms of explosive hazards and remnants of war (unexploded and abandoned ordnance) also had to be addressed. A later focus on cluster munitions as a specifically significant threat resulted in a further modification of the scope of mine action. The need to develop effective treaties and laws may have both reflected and driven the dynamic evolution of mine action. A well-defined legal framework emerged, with three principal instruments of international law:

- Convention on Certain Conventional Weapons (CCW), with its Amended Protocol II and Protocol V;
- Anti-Personnel Mine Ban Convention (APMBC);
- Convention on Cluster Munitions (CCM).

The first treaty addressing contamination by explosive hazards is the UN's CCW,[38] which forms a framework treaty applicable to situations of armed conflict containing generic provisions and protocols relating to specific weapons and their use. It is built upon the customary rules that regulate the conduct of hostilities contained in international humanitarian law (IHL), including the principle of distinction between combatants and civilians; proportionality between the choice of military targets and the intended military objectives; precautions in attacks; and prohibition of weapons that are of a nature to inflict superfluous injury or suffering on combatants.[39] In 1980 states adopted the framework convention and its first three protocols.

Protocol II on Landmines, Booby-Traps and Other Devices reflected the state of customary law at that time by limiting the use of landmines, booby-traps and "other devices" and requiring some general measures to be taken to reduce the dangers to civilians. However, the rules were later shown to provide inadequate protection to civilians from the effects of anti-personnel mines in particular, and in 1996 the High Contracting Parties amended the protocol; it now further regulates but does not ban the use of landmines, booby-traps and other explosive devices. Under Protocol V on Explosive Remnants of War, adopted in 2003, states recognize the serious problems caused by ERW and commit to take remedial measures and all feasible precautions to minimize their occurrence and impact.

Although the 1996 amendment to CCW Protocol II fell short of prohibiting landmines, civil society and pro-ban states took advantage of the momentum generated. They initiated a new process outside the UN framework, which concluded in a global ban on anti-personnel mines with the adoption of the APMBC[40] in 1997. The convention entered into force in 1999, with the clear humanitarian goal of putting an end to civilian suffering from anti-personnel mines. To achieve this, the convention establishes an absolute ban on the production, use, transfer and stockpiling of anti-personnel mines. In addition, it requires remedial measures such as the destruction of stockpiles, clearance of emplaced mines and support to victims. The APMBC has become the backbone of mine action and, with the inclusion of victim assistance, initiated a ground-breaking normative development. As of January 2016, 162 countries have agreed to be bound by the APMBC, and many that have not done so do abide by its main principles and objectives.

In 2006 negotiations on cluster munitions were initiated within the CCW. In parallel, liked-minded states started a process reminiscent in several aspects of the negotiations which led to the APMBC.[41] This process concluded with the adoption of the CCM in 2008 and its subsequent entry into force in 2010. The CCM comprehensively prohibits the production, use, transfer and stockpiling of cluster munitions, and requires the destruction of stockpiled cluster munitions and the clearance of their remnants. It also contains detailed provisions on victim assistance. As of January 2016, a total of 98 states have ratified or acceded to the CCM.

In addition to the conventions, mine action is regulated by IMAS. Although not legally binding, they provide guidance to mine action stakeholders and translate the principles included in IHL treaties, basic human rights and clearance requirements into practical and detailed norms. IMAS have become the relevant standards implemented by mine action organizations, and constitute the basis for national mine action standards. Mine action further relies where relevant on the 2011 International Ammunition Technical Guidelines (IATG), providing standards for the management and destruction of ammunition stockpiles, and the 2012 International Small Arms Control Standards (ISACS). These two norms reflect the trend in mine action to broaden its support to include ammunition and SALW.

The various international treaties and standards lay a solid normative foundation, the extent of which might be missing for SSR. It is demonstrated below that the international obligations and IMAS provide useful guidance for the implementation of mine action, for instance in relation to good governance and the adoption of a human-rights-based approach.

Initially conceived as a humanitarian emergency response, mine action's focus was on safely and efficiently removing the threat of mines, cluster munitions and ERW to meet basic security needs of the civilian population and humanitarian workers. While this remains a key priority, it has been increasingly recognized in recent years that explosive legacies of armed conflict also impede the construction of infrastructure required for economic activity and mobility, and limit access to resources (e.g. water and land) and social services (e.g. schools and clinics).

Figure 2: Mine action programme stages[42]

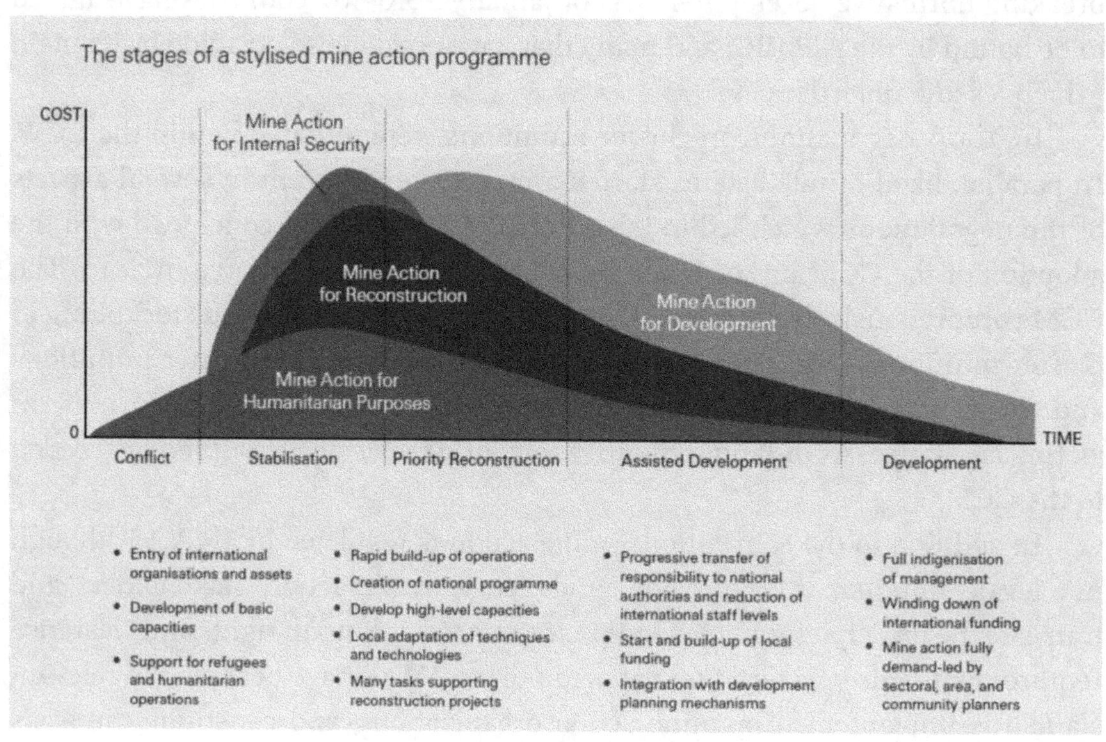

Hence, beyond the immediate humanitarian concern, the importance of mine action for and its broader contribution to a country's longer-term peacebuilding and development have enjoyed greater attention. This trend is illustrated schematically in Figure 2, representing the stylized transition stages of a mine action programme over time from conflict to stabilization, reconstruction and longer-term development. Mine action organizations and donors have started to place an increasing emphasis on ensuring that mine action achieves developmental outcomes such as access to basic services and improved livelihoods.[43]

Another evolution of mine action relates to activities which organizations undertake beyond their traditional mandate. Although there are diverging views on whether such activities fall within core mine action,[44] or if they rather represent related fields with which mine action organizations increasingly interact, the trend whereby mine action organizations address broader threats to safety and security is uncontested.[45]

Threats to safety and security are globally understood in a wider – and widening – context, recognizing in part the broad threats of armed violence to human security. Drawing on their longstanding experience, technical expertise and capacities in removing and destroying mines and ERW in a wide range of conflict and post-conflict contexts, mine action organizations have in some cases evolved towards addressing other instruments of violence, such as SALW and ammunition, or even towards engaging with the agents of violence.

As conflicts evolve, mine action organizations respond dynamically to emerging challenges, such as the increased use of improvised explosive devices (IEDs). As a weapon of choice for non-state armed groups, IEDs are used against military personnel, peacekeepers and civilians alike. Poorly secured and inadequately managed ammunition sites can fuel the production of IEDs and, as the UN Security Council expressed in Resolution 2040 (2012) on Libya, proliferation of weapons and explosives poses a serious risk to regional and international security.[46] In addition, improperly managed storage areas with ageing ammunition represent a considerable humanitarian hazard, as testified by the number of unplanned explosions in depots located in populated areas, causing widespread damage to people and infrastructure.[47]

Therefore, mine action operators increasingly engage in physical security and stockpile management (PSSM) programmes, entailing mainly training in accounting and munitions handling practices to enhance theft prevention, deterrence measures, demilitarization and refurbishing or building new storage depots.[48]

This ongoing evolution of mine action actors towards addressing wider security threats related to issues such as IEDs and munition stockpiles is largely in response to observed needs on the ground and in recognition of increased efficiency and effectiveness if the problem is addressed in a more comprehensive manner. Hence not only has SSR become more holistic, but so have mine action actors. The following subsection examines how peacekeeping and peacebuilding relate to a broadened understanding of security, and how their evolution gave rise to SSR and mine action becoming essential tasks in such contexts.

The evolution of peacekeeping and peacebuilding

SSR and mine action do not take place exclusively in post-conflict countries, but their definition and evolution are fundamentally connected with the promotion of peace. For this reason, this subsection shows that the broadening of the *modus operandi* of UN peacekeeping and political/peacebuilding missions is instrumental in identifying existing and potential interactions between SSR and mine action and grasping the importance of linking them in post-conflict contexts.

UN peacekeeping has evolved since its beginning. Traditional peacekeeping was a tool for conflict management and relied on three principles: consent of the parties to the conflict, neutrality and impartiality, and use of force for self-defence or in defence of the mandate. This approach has been undermined by the rise of intrastate conflicts and the targeting of civilian populations, violations of human rights and IHL, and the multiplication of actors involved in a conflict. Thus traditional peacekeeping has been largely replaced by multi-dimensional peacekeeping operations that have a wider spectrum of activities, including facilitation of national political dialogues and reconciliation, protection of civilians, support to elections, DDR processes and the restoration of the rule of law.[49] In addition, some missions have become more "robust", as illustrated by the establishment of the Intervention Brigade within the UN Organization Stabilization Mission in the Democratic Republic of the Congo (MONUSCO).[50] According to Ramsbothan et al., this pattern reflects an effort "to expand the traditional concept of military *collective security* ... into an international commitment to use military force, where required, ultimately under a UN aegis, to uphold the wider concept of *human security*".[51]

The broader spectrum of peacekeeping activities provides an overlap between peacekeeping and post-conflict peacebuilding in the first phases of a peace process, because multidimensional peacekeeping is supposed to play a "catalytic role" in favour of peacebuilding (see Figure 3).[52]

Figure 3: Linkages and grey areas[53]

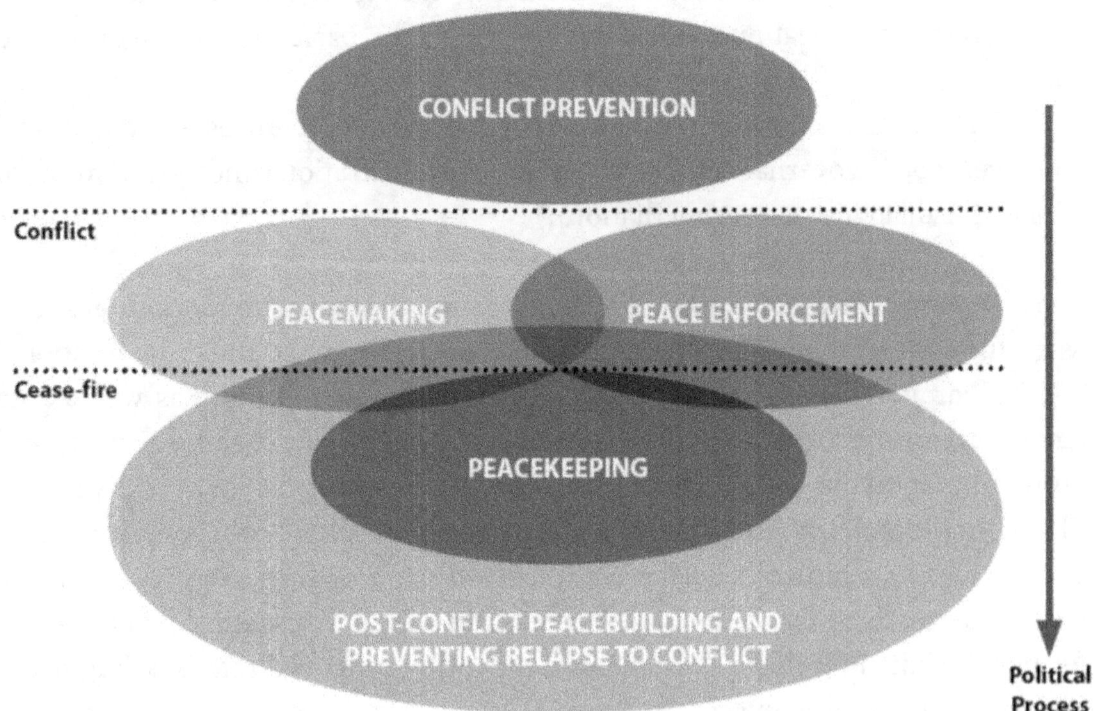

The concept of peacebuilding was defined in the 1992 "Agenda for peace" as a response to the evolution and limits of traditional peacekeeping as described above. Boutros-Ghali's agenda perceived peacebuilding as an action linearly following conflict prevention, peacemaking and peacekeeping by defining it as an "action to identify and support structures which tend to strengthen and solidify peace to avoid relapse into conflict".[54]

Peacebuilding as a concept evolved and was refined during the 1990s to become better integrated. More than two decades later the UN has initiated several major reviews of its capacities for conflict prevention and peacebuilding, and while the implications of these reviews remain as yet unclear, it is likely that a closer analysis of the linkages between peacebuilding activities will be required.[55] Since 2001, the Security Council has understood the aim of peacebuilding as "preventing the outbreak, the recurrence or continuation of armed conflict and therefore [it] encompasses a wide range of political, developmental, humanitarian and human rights programmes and mechanisms".[56] Despite its many challenges, the immediate aftermath of conflict provides unique peacebuilding opportunities in three mutually reinforcing dimensions:

- basic safety and security (such as through mine action, protection of civilians, DDR, strengthening the rule of law and SSR);
- socio-economic peace dividends (including the provision of basic services, economic revitalization and rehabilitation of basic infrastructure and employment);
- political reconstruction and processes (including electoral processes, transitional justice, good governance, basic public administration and promotion of inclusive dialogue and reconciliation).[57]

The evolution of peacekeeping and the emergence of peacebuilding came at a time when the concept of and discourse on human security gained much international political support. The trends in peacekeeping and peacebuilding as well as the emergence of the human security approach responded to the same security and humanitarian challenges and to the changing nature of conflict in the early 1990s. The thematic and time congruencies clearly suggest that the conceptualization of and narrative on human security reflected and supported the way in which the UN rethought its peace operations. Although anecdotal, it is symptomatic that the former Canadian foreign minister Lloyd Axworthy proposed that building peace is about building human security.[58]

Human security is especially relevant to peace operations when bearing in mind that peacekeeping and special political missions (also referred to as political/peacebuilding missions in this paper) are more and more required to link security and development efforts. What is more, a common pattern of intrastate conflict is the targeting of civilians. The trend underlines a need to focus on the human impact of conflict and the adequacy of a human security approach to peacekeeping.[59] The question of whether stable peace can be achieved without ensuring human security at individual and community level is of course, simple as it might seem, of particular relevance.[60]

The converging evolution of peacekeeping and peacebuilding missions in conjunction with the dominant role of the human security concept prompted the inclusion of SSR and mine action as essential elements in such missions. While the Security Council had earlier been involved in tasks related to SSR support and implicitly referred to SSR, it has given peacekeeping and political missions explicit SSR mandates only since 2004.[61] This shift reflects the interconnected nature of SSR, increasingly recognized since the late 1990s in line with the evolving understanding of peacekeeping and peacebuilding in the sense that political, economic, legal, social and security sector reforms have to be undertaken holistically to meet the security needs of individuals and communities in post-conflict peace operations.[62]

Similarly, mine action components have been introduced in many peacekeeping missions.[63] More explicitly, the UN Security Council noted in 2003 the importance of addressing mine action in mandates for peacekeeping operations.[64] That same year, through restructuring its mine action coordination center, the UN Mission in Ethiopia and Eritrea became effectively the first peacekeeping mission to incorporate an integrated civilian and military mine action headquarters in the mission structure.[65] A review of current mandates is provided in the third section of this paper.

As for other peacebuilding activities, SSR and mine action support the prevention of violent conflict and peacebuilding in its three dimensions listed above. Their contribution to basic safety and security may be the most visible.[66] Mine action seeks to provide physical safety, for example through clearance of contaminated areas or the reduction of stockpiled weapons and ammunition.[67] SSR aims to ensure that security provision is locally owned, accountable and effective, thereby contributing to building confidence in and strengthening state institutions, as well as to enhancing the rule of law and the security apparatus protecting the population.

The contribution of SSR and mine action to peacebuilding also entails dividends for socio-economic development. Addressing the various peacebuilding dimensions simultaneously and in a balanced way is a challenge in post-conflict peacebuilding, but a necessity, since it is widely admitted that "there can be no peace without development, no development without peace, and no lasting peace or sustainable development without respect for human rights and the rule of law".[68] Thus it is often argued that an appropriately sized, accountable and well-governed security sector contributes to an environment less prone to violence, thereby improving both security and sustainable economic and human development.[69] This refers to an even broader and demonstrated link that governance and effectiveness not only foster development but at the same time reduce the potential for conflict.[70]

Interestingly, the debate on SSR in the early 1990s started among development donors looking at ways to improve the effectiveness of development aid. The positive effects of SSR in terms of improved safety of people and property, a shift of expenditures from military to development, conflict prevention and wider participation in decision-making on security provision came up very prominently in the discussions.[71] However, the concrete developmental impact of SSR is subject to controversy. While it is assumed that the above objectives are at the core of SSR, it is less obvious that SSR has thus far been programmed with development goals in mind.[72] In post-conflict situations it is apparent that SSR's security mandate has been more vigorously pursued than its development dividends.[73]

The contribution of mine action to development is more obvious. Contamination by or fear of ERW leads to human displacement, delays the return and resettlement of refugees and internally displaced persons, and blocks access to vital resources and social services.[74] In response to the recognition of this clear interconnectedness, mine action organizations and their donors started to place increasing emphasis on the "security–development nexus" and integrate mine action into broader national development plans.[75]

Finally, some scholars and practitioners point to the primacy of the political aspect of peacebuilding,[76] which SSR supports very directly. It is more difficult to demonstrate mine action's contribution to the political dimension of peacebuilding, especially given the fact that in most instances traditional mine action has a humanitarian vocation. What is uncontested, however, is that mine action can play a key role in confidence building among warring parties, including through sharing information about minefields and conducting joint demining projects. This may serve as a foundation for conflict resolution or inject valuable confidence in the peace process with spin-off effects on reconciliation. With populations seeing enemies or former parties to the conflict clearing and removing the explosive hazards affecting them, confidence can be built or rebuilt.

To sum up, SSR and mine action evolved from a narrow set of activities to more comprehensive action, and this evolution is grounded in a changing understanding of security. Also, the emergence of the human security concept is reflected in the evolution from traditional to multidimensional peacekeeping and the growing emphasis on integrated peacebuilding. This contributed to the explicit conceptual inclusion of SSR and mine action in such missions. An understanding of this broadened perspective on security proves essential to examining the conceptual commonalities between SSR and mine action, which are the focus of the following section.

SSR and Mine Action: Common Approaches

The previous section describes the general pattern of the broadening understanding of the concept of security beyond the sole security of the state. This change is related to the development of the concept of human security and reflected in how SSR, mine action and peacekeeping/building operations are defined today. This section takes a step further by showing that SSR and mine action not only share the same understanding of security, but also have strong similarities in the way programmes should be designed and implemented.

In particular, this section examines in greater depth approaches common to both SSR and mine action, and scrutinizes how these commonalities are articulated conceptually. This analysis prepares the ground for the third section, in which these conceptual linkages are tested against the operational realities. We identify national ownership and capacity development, good governance and a people-centred focus and human rights as shared approaches given their cross-cutting nature and relevance to SSR and mine action. They further reflect some of the founding elements of human security as defined in the first section.

National ownership and capacity development

SSR and mine action are steered by the assumption that concerned states bear the ultimate responsibility for both processes. There is recognition that for SSR and mine action to be successful and sustainable, national ownership[77] is *sine qua non* and commitment by national leadership indispensable.[78]

The legal-normative framework governing mine action is helpful in this regard, as it makes state responsibility a legal obligation. For instance, the APMBC and CCM confer responsibility on concerned states very explicitly, noting their obligation to destroy stockpiles and clear the territory under their jurisdiction or control. Likewise, IMAS enshrine this principle, stipulating that the primary responsibility is vested in the government of the mine-affected state.[79]

The importance of national ownership is also key for SSR. United Nations Security Council Resolution 2151(2014) "reiterates the centrality" of national ownership of SSR and "the responsibility of the country concerned in the determination of security sector reform assistance".[80] Yet because SSR targets the reorganization of political power structures and authority, SSR might be an endeavour with greater political implications than mine action. National ownership of SSR might thus be more sensitive, since it involves issues related to accountability and control. Hence, given such implications, national motivations for reform may not always align with the good governance principles promoted by SSR processes. What is more, aid providers could fear that their support to the security sector might be misused to commit human rights violations.[81]

Armed conflict generally leads to a lack of governance institutions or weak and even illegitimate structures. In this context, national ownership might be illusory in an early phase and external assistance is usually provided to ensure the delivery of the most critical peacekeeping and peacebuilding tasks, including SSR and mine action. While some authors caution the risk of aid dependency potentially leading to reduced efforts of recipient countries to help themselves and an inherent tension between externally induced, funded and supported initiatives and national ownership, such an institutional vacuum also provides excellent opportunities for setting up effective and accountable structures and building the necessary capacities from the outset.[82]

It is often noted that a precise definition of national ownership in SSR contexts is challenging, due to the very different environments in which SSR is undertaken and the varying "stages" at which reforming states find themselves, especially post-conflict. In the same vein, the level of support needed by affected states in mine action is uneven: some programmes only require limited external assistance, building on solid national know-how and institutions, while others request more profound support. Leaning on Nathan's conceptualization, the objective of national ownership might in both cases be that the mine action programme or the reform of security policies, institutions and projects is designed, managed and implemented by domestic, not external, actors.[83]

With the involvement of international stakeholders such as the UN, international or regional organizations and NGOs at the early stage of post-conflict recovery, the issue of transitioning responsibilities to national entities is therefore a critical, although delicate, process. In mine action this role is generally assumed by the UN Mine Action Service (UNMAS), which manages temporarily – sometimes for years – a national programme while striving to accelerate the transfer of responsibilities to national actors at an appropriate time.[84] However, transition has to be well timed so as to ensure that the capacities, institutions and structures are in place and sustainable. Transition can only take place and responsibilities be assumed if there is a progressive "handover" process "through which the international community reduces its financial and technical support, as the affected state develops the required national programme management capacities that lead to national ownership. Successful transition will only occur when these parallel components have been reasonably effective."[85]

This definition entails building and developing national capacities to ensure that they are capable, empowered and adequately equipped to assume ownership. In post-conflict environments, however, the development of national capacities is often addressed as part of exit strategies of international interventions, whereas it should be an integral part thereof immediately at the outset. Both SSR and mine action actors face this challenge. This concern becomes particularly striking when keeping in mind that "inattention to capacity development constrains national actors from taking ownership of their recovery and limits accountability between the State and its people".[86]

In mine action in particular, experience illustrates that it can be challenging to accommodate donor preferences for home-grown organizations and in-kind contributions, since this external support might not be the most appropriate in a given environment.[87] In the same vein, Donais stresses a different, but related, challenge in SSR – equally relevant to mine action – with regards to political will from donors. Putting the concept of national ownership into practice requires donors to cede parts of the control and authority they usually tend to exert and accept a higher level of uncertainty.[88] The issue of the willingness of donor states to lose part of their sovereignty over aid provision is, however, a more systemic challenge which also emerges in broader debates on donor coordination and aid effectiveness.[89]

Good governance: Transparency, accountability and effectiveness

Another conceptual commonality between SSR and mine action relates to good governance. Good governance has been interpreted by development donors as a concept aimed at improving the efficiency and effectiveness of public services. It is widely understood to be composed of three key pillars: accountability; transparency, interpreted as freely available information, therefore representing a precondition for accountability and sound decision-making; and participation of citizens, either directly or through legitimate intermediaries such as parliamentary representatives.[90]

SSR seeks to apply the principles of good governance to the security sector to ensure that individuals and societies feel safer through more effective and accountable security provision. In this context, it is critical that security institutions work under civilian control and the rule of law, since the absence of accountability, resulting in an environment where security institutions can act with impunity, may often lead to political interference and human rights violations. The absence of accountability puts human security at risk.[91] In turn, SSR favours security institutions under civilian oversight and democratic governance, gives people a participative voice in the decision-making process regarding security institutions and promotes a legitimate, transparent and inclusive state which is accountable to its citizens. SSR therefore has a substantive role to play in consolidating democracy and promoting human rights.[92] Indeed, rights holders are not simply reliant on the good will of the state to deliver rights, but should participate actively in developing and implementing policies that provide for those rights.[93]

However, "providing both security and democratic governance is not an easy challenge to meet".[94] Particularly in post-conflict peacebuilding, it is of utmost importance to enhance good governance in the security sector, even though a common error in programming usually gives less priority to the promotion of transparency and democratic accountability than to training and equipping security forces.[95]

The three key good governance pillars also apply to humanitarian demining. Since mine action re-establishes access to vital resources, prioritization of tasks is an essential element of these programmes. During such processes a number of aspects have to be taken into account, such as land rights, political and social considerations and development perspectives. With a view to not doing harm nor creating or refuelling tensions, a legitimate, participatory and transparent process is required which will ultimately enhance good governance and ensure the enjoyment of human rights.[96] The importance of participation in strategic planning is also essential to this goal as stressed in a recent study on this issue.[97] This clearly reflects the wider recognition that active participation from the population is the basis for any successful peace process. Furthermore, dialogue on security issues should be carried out with a gender and diversity perspective, as security might be perceived differently by women, girls, boys and men, as well as minority groups.[98] Broad participation fosters ownership and the inclusion of local context and specificities.

Mine action is often among the first internationally supported mechanisms in post-conflict environments. As such, it is a good entry point to promote good governance, with considerable spin-off effects on further structures in the security sector established at a later stage. There can be a time lapse between SSR and mine action given the different phases of conflict when they begin, which can lead to some difficulties in linking the two sets of activities.[99] Yet the potential for mine action to influence broader governance practices is still recognized.[100]

Although each operational environment is different and a context-specific needs assessment is required, mine action may be more straightforward in terms of the possible institutional architecture than SSR. IMAS provide guidance on governance for regulating, managing and coordinating mine action, so the necessary institutions are put in place for states to assume ownership. IMAS generally suggest a division of responsibilities between a mostly interministerial national mine action authority in charge of policy, regulation and the overall management of mine action programmes and a national mine action centre that has essentially an executive role.[101] An example of a recommended national mine action structure is set out in Figure 4.

Figure 4: Mine action institutions[102]

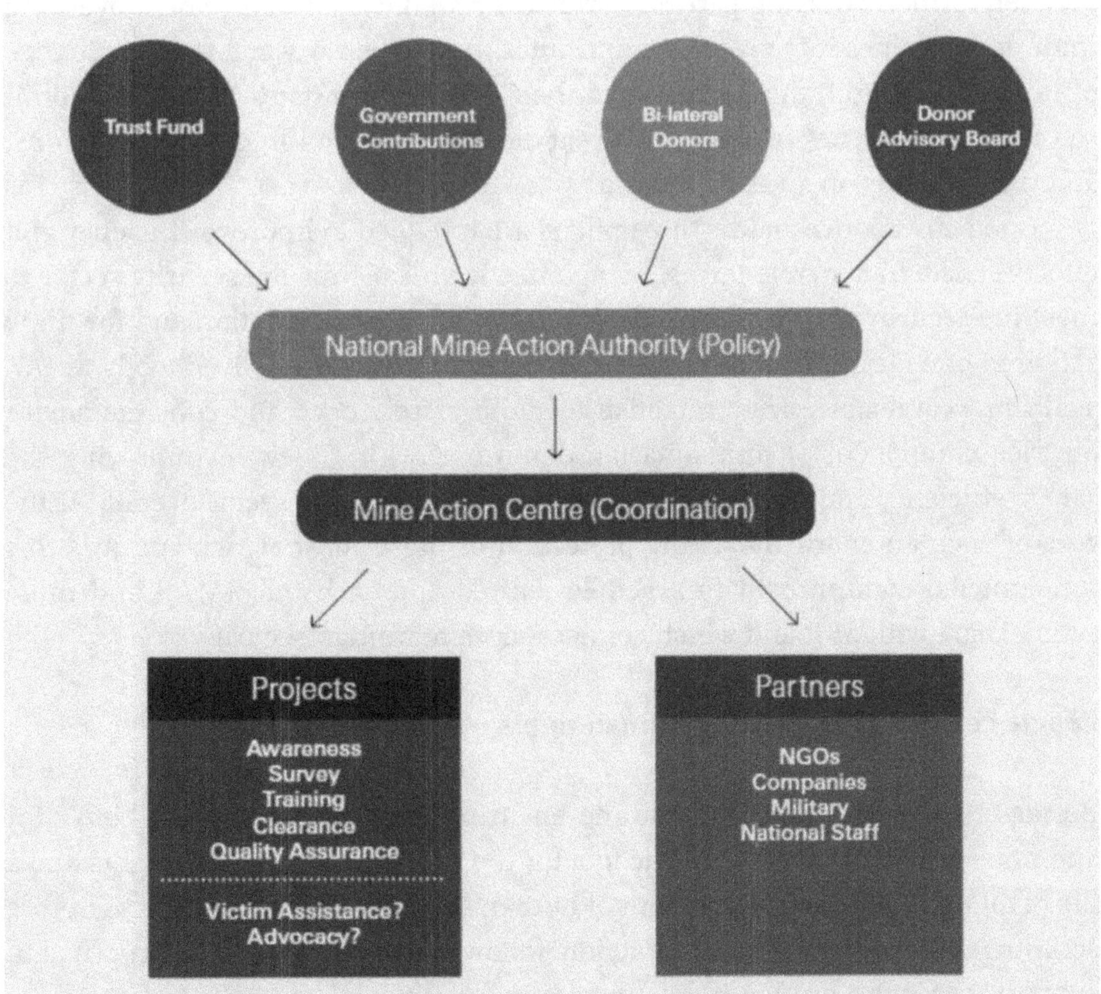

An unequivocal and transparent institutional architecture with clear responsibilities, checks and balances is a precondition for institutions to be accountable. The set-up of institutions rests upon legal instruments, mostly national legislation, preceded by a political process involving government, parliament and agencies and offering excellent opportunities for inclusive participation. Ultimately, this kind of legislation is the source of legitimacy for mine action institutions and programmes. Accountability is further ensured in the sense that national mine action authorities generally report to parliaments.[103]

On a cautionary note, Bryden stipulates that the set-up of internationally funded mine action capacities may also lead to corruption and self-interest, hence it is important to streamline parallel efforts to increase effectiveness within oversight mechanisms.[104] The development of mine action institutions is a good example of potentially fruitful synergies between SSR and mine action. SSR could – or should – provide an analytical framework and expertise helping to understand the overall institutional security architecture and political dimension of mine action, as well as to identify critical issues and design possible solutions.

Finally, transparency is key for mine action to serve as a confidence builder between formerly warring parties. In this context, the legal framework governing mine action comes into play and contributes to transparency and to the exchange of information. Both the APMBC and the CCM require States Parties to submit so-called transparency reports, initially at the moment of joining the conventions, and subsequently on an annual basis.[105]

Good governance and its three pillars are intended to improve efficiency and effectiveness. In concrete terms, being effective means for the security sector to meet the security and justice needs of the state and its population and for mine action to provide a safe and secure environment and access to livelihoods. IMAS again prove valuable. They establish a frame of reference and concrete advice on each component of humanitarian demining, with a view to improving the safety, efficiency and effectiveness of programmes and the sector overall. At the core of such an endeavour is the protection of those most at risk and it is this fundamental commitment to a people-centred approach that IMAS and mine action share with SSR and which connects both to human security.

People-centred approach and human rights

Besides their ties to development and ensuring freedom from want, both SSR and mine action serve as a catalytic tool for the promotion of human rights and a life of dignity – another key element of human security. This subsection therefore scrutinizes how SSR and mine action follow a people-centred approach and support respect for human rights, including equality.

The link between SSR and human rights is of particular importance and relevance due to the fact that SSR mostly takes place in countries in which the security sector may have been a major threat to the human rights of their people and protectors have become perpetrators of human rights abuses. In the aftermath of conflict, security stakeholders can be feared and mistrusted by the population in an environment of impunity in which security forces are not held accountable. Despite these circumstances, the state bears the principal responsibility for international obligations such as human rights law. In addition to stopping direct violations of human rights, the state is required to create an environment conducive to the enjoyment of internationally agreed human rights by its people. Since the traditional security sector plays a central role in ensuring the protection of such rights, a post-conflict state cannot simply rely on a historically abusive security sector. To do nothing in such circumstances may be considered as an omission, and hence a wrongful act.[106]

At a policy level the linkages are clearly outlined, such as in the OECD-DAC SSR handbook where the strengthening of respect for human rights is considered to be a key principle of SSR.[107] It is less clear, though, what exactly a state is required to do under international law in relation to reforming its security sector, and not much analysis is available on how SSR programming should actually be informed by human rights in terms of legal duty. International law does, however, provide principles to steer SSR work: the duty to respect and ensure human rights must entail due diligence to analyse patterns of abuse; states must investigate gross violations of human rights law and serious violations of IHL and prosecute perpetrators; and states must ensure that the victims' rights are guaranteed. These obligations underline the centrality of human rights training and vetting, among others, and should clarify the objectives of SSR programming.[108] In the same vein, a human rights approach emphasizes the relationship between the rights holders and the duty-bearer, while trying to adjust institutions or laws to make sure that the duty-bearer – the state – actually fulfils its obligations. According to Galletti and Wodzicki, this could mean in practice that SSR may need to shift from a state-capacity paradigm to a state-obligation paradigm.[109]

In the context of UN peace operations, missions are required to apply the UN's Human Rights Due Diligence Policy, which "sets out measures that all United Nations entities must take in order to ensure that any support that they may provide to non-United Nations forces is consistent with the purposes and principles as set out in the Charter of the United Nations and with its responsibility to respect, promote and encourage respect for international humanitarian, human rights and refugee law."[110] The due diligence policy requires UN entities to assess whether security forces receiving support are already engaged in or are likely to commit grave violations of international humanitarian, human rights or refugee law; and, where this may be the case to work with relevant authorities to stop the abuses or ultimately end support. Applying the due diligence policy has provided an initial basis for a human-rights approach to SSR in the context of UN support even if much remains to be improved in this area.

The importance of a comprehensive approach to SSR in relation to human rights might be best illustrated by the 2012 report of the Special Rapporteur of the Human Rights Council on the promotion of truth, justice, reparation and guarantees of non-recurrence in the context of transitional justice. Accordingly, transitional justice should, for instance, include institutional reform or vetting of office holders with a view to ensuring non-recurrence of human rights violations.[111] This demonstrates the direct contribution of SSR to the respect for and promotion of human rights and the need for these linkages to be institutionalized, as proposed by the Special Rapporteur. In fact, should abusive security officials not be held accountable and simply recycled into reformed security forces as part of SSR and/ or DDR processes, the right to reparations and the state's duty to ensure respect of international rights can hardly be upheld, while the legitimacy of the security sector – paramount for its effectiveness – continues to be eroded. According to some scholars, though, while the importance of human rights training and vetting is recognized in SSR at policy level, they are not necessarily understood as being driven by international legal obligations.[112] Hence, as Galletti and Wodzicki articulate it, "by shifting the paradigm of SSR to a human rights perspective, SSR becomes part of the process to secure human rights".[113]

Good governance and transparency are also critical to ensure economic and social rights. Excessive military budgets can draw badly needed resources away from humanitarian or development projects and may impede a state in realizing internationally protected rights. By promoting civilian control and transparency within the security sector, SSR can prevent or counteract such situations. Economic and social rights can also be violated directly by security forces, for instance through corruption. SSR again plays a determinant role in creating an environment in which the state can address effectively questions of corruption or other forms of economic violence.[114] It is therefore essential that a human rights framework focuses on accountability, without which laws are powerless. This is certainly as valid for SSR as it is for mine action.

Mine action follows a human-rights-based approach, given that mines and ERW can directly affect the exercise of a number of political, economic, social, civil and cultural rights. Without being exhaustive, these include the right to life and security of a person, the right to an adequate standard of living and the right to education, all enshrined in the Universal Declaration of Human Rights. The relevance of mine action to respect for the right to food can be exemplified by the report of the Special Rapporteur on food after his mission to Lebanon in 2006, which demonstrates how mine/ERW contamination can severely decrease the ability of affected populations to feed themselves through an adequate livelihood.[115]

Mine action and the removal of contamination by mines and ERW may also drastically improve the enjoyment of the freedom of movement.[116] Hence any concrete mine action project on the ground contributes to re-establishing the exercise of an array of internationally guaranteed rights. A founding principle for the development of IMAS consisted in protecting those most at risk, which underscores the strong people-centred – and consequently human security – focus of mine action.

In this context, assistance to victims merits particular emphasis. The first section of this paper redrew the evolution of mine action and the international legal framework surrounding it; within this, the rights of persons with disabilities, in particular victims,[117] have gained increasing attention, not least because of the landmark provisions of the APMBC.[118] For the first time, legal obligations to assist victims of a particular weapons system were included in an international instrument governing conventional weapons.[119] It also expanded the traditional understanding of state responsibility, with states accepting that they have important human security and human rights responsibilities.[120]

The CCW's Protocol V and the CCM subsequently embodied similar provisions, with the CCM especially going beyond the APMBC requirements.[121] Since the ultimate objective is to achieve the full and effective participation of victims in society on an equal basis with others, this requires the integration of victim assistance into broader contexts such as disability rights, health and employment.[122] In this regard, the entry into force of the UN Convention on the Rights of Persons with Disabilities further boosted the attention given to victims by clarifying states' obligation to ensure the equal enjoyment of human rights by persons with disabilities. As such, mine action serves in the application and promotion of human rights instruments.

Especially the APMBC and the CCM provide a useful framework and guidance for the concrete implementation of human-rights-based assistance to victims. Beyond the obligations they contain, five-year action plans go into much more detail about actions required by States Parties. Not only do such plans ensure progress in victim assistance, but each review conference at which the international community takes stock of achievements also helps demonstrate the realism of state responsibility for victims.[123] As an example, the APMBC States Parties committed in the 2014–2019 Maputo Action Plan to communicate "time-bound and measurable objectives [they seek] to achieve through the implementation of national policies, plans and legal frameworks that will tangibly contribute, to the full, equal and effective participation of mine victims in society".[124]

Therefore, while both SSR and mine action have adopted a human-rights-based approach which could still be strengthened, mine action – unlike SSR – can rely on international legal norms and agreed actions which have embraced this approach. Yet despite this difference in the development of international legal frameworks, both sectors adhere to the principle that a human rights framework helps to secure freedoms and human development and to empower people to take part in the decisions that will affect their lives.

For empowerment of people to be truly meaningful, the participation and inclusion of the society in its entirety on an equal basis and without discrimination is a precondition. Gender and diversity are therefore relevant to SSR and mine action. In his first report on SSR, the UN Secretary-General stressed that a gender approach "is key to developing security sector institutions that are non-discriminatory, representative of the population and capable of effectively responding to the specific security needs of diverse groups".[125] This is based on the recognition that women, girls, boys and men as well as minority groups experience security and insecurity in different ways. Likewise, the OECD-DAC SSR handbook underscores that the comprehensive integration of gender equality dimensions into SSR is of central importance to ensure local ownership, oversight, accountability and not least effective provision of security.[126]

Improved inclusion of women and marginalized groups can be supported, for example, by their participation in SSR planning or through structural reforms targeting personnel practices (e.g. recruitment).[127] Inclusive security sector institutions, which represent the diversity of societies at large are more likely to be trusted and perceived as legitimate, as well as more effective in their mission but these benefits require the security forces be appropriately diverse and representative in their composition.[128] The need to develop gender- and identity- specific indicators and to collect disaggregated data is thus given high priority in SSR.

On the mine action side, as for SSR, elements such as inclusive planning, recruitment practices and collecting and analysing disaggregated data are cross-cutting and, as for SSR, conducive to improved effectiveness in programmes. It is therefore not surprising that the well-developed legal-normative framework in mine action provides a powerful awareness of gender and diversity requirements. Indeed, a gender and diversity lens has been embedded in, for instance, the CCM and the Maputo Action Plan, and emphasizes the need for gender-sensitive clearance, MRE and victim assistance.[129] Furthermore, IMAS specify more detailed requirements for a gender and diversity perspective in all aspects of mine action, including planning, implementation and monitoring.

Concretely, disaggregation of information by identity categories, including gender and age, enhances the prioritization and planning of mine action work and allows activities, including MRE, to be tailored according to gender-specific exposure to risk and mobility patterns.[130] Moreover, as in SSR, employment and training opportunities in mine action should be provided to women and men without discrimination. In many cultures it is not appropriate for women to interact with men outside their immediate families. Having women and men working in survey teams (tasked with collecting information from affected communities regarding the location of mines/ERW), for example, is essential, since it enables them to access and reach out to affected women and girls and make information-gathering processes more effective. This enhances the effectiveness, accountability and responsiveness of mine action and the same principles also apply to the work of the security sector more broadly.

Armed conflict can both catalyse change in gender norms and entrench discrimination. Ultimately, both SSR and mine action strive to change mentalities and institutional cultures, promoting equality and ensuring that entrenched discrimination is not perpetuated in a post-conflict environment or a reformed security sector.[131] SSR and mine action can be inclusive and effective only when meeting the differing security needs of all people. There are clear gender- and diversity-related linkages between SSR and mine action, as the key principles of gender mainstreaming and equal participation of all social groups apply to both fields.

In sum, this section shows that some of the foundational elements of human security as defined in the first section are translated into principles that shape the SSR and mine action approaches to programme design and implementation. In particular, there are strong conceptual commonalities between SSR and mine action related to national ownership and capacity development, good governance, a people-centred focus and human rights. These cross-cutting approaches provide for substantive overlap between how SSR and mine action are conceptualized. Because of these overlaps it could be expected that linking SSR and mine action in operational terms would offer enhanced opportunities to improve good governance, protect human rights and provide for human security. Yet to date, mine action and SSR have developed as discrete areas of operational and policy interest with relatively few efforts made to operationalize the conceptual linkages between the two agendas. The following section examines to what extent these conceptual linkages are reflected in operational terms and what might be gained from drawing them closer together.

Operationalizing Linkages between SSR and Mine Action

This section examines whether the conceptual commonalities between SSR and mine action so far discussed are operationalized in the field. It first looks at UN peacekeeping and political/peacebuilding missions, as they play a critical role in conducting SSR and mine action in post-conflict environments. In particular, it enquires how frequently SSR and mine action are in the mandates of these missions and whether there is a significant connection between them. Subsequently, the section broadens its perspective by considering examples of SSR and mine action beyond UN missions, because bilateral programmes implemented by states or NGOs also play an important role in post-conflict peacebuilding and may provide further evidence of how the conceptual commonalities between the two fields are translated into practice.

SSR and mine action in the mandates of UN peacekeeping missions

As shown in the first section, UN peacekeeping missions have become integrated and multidimensional and play a "catalytic role" in favour of important peacebuilding activities, including SSR and mine action. As of August 2015, a review of the current peacekeeping and special political missions[132] shows that out of 25 missions, 14 mandates contain tasks related to SSR, eight are peacekeeping missions and six are political/peacebuilding missions. Among the 25 missions, 14 also have an explicit or implicit[133] reference to mine action activities in their mandates. Finally, ten missions have tasks in both SSR and mine action.

Table 1: Overview of peacekeeping and political/peacebuilding missions[134]

	Number of missions	Chapter VI UN Charter	Chapter VII UN Charter	SSR explicit	SSR implicit	Mine action explicit	Mine action implicit	SSR and mine action
Peacekeeping missions	16	6	10	6	2	7	4	7
Special political/ peacebuilding missions	9	0	2	4	2	2	1	3
Total	25	6	12	10	4	9	5	10

These figures substantiate the claim that the conceptual overlaps between SSR and mine action translate directly into operational contexts. Closer examination reveals the concrete issues on which SSR and mine action do—and do not—interact.

Starting with the peacekeeping missions, eight have a mandate in SSR and all are stabilization missions (see Table 2). Six have explicit tasks in SSR that consist mainly of assisting the re-establishment and/or strengthening of a state's institutions through advice and coordination of other international efforts in SSR. Often, SSR activities are related to a peace agreement, which provides the objective of the reforms and the specific security sector components that have to be reformed. For instance, the UN Mission in Mali (MINUSMA) is tasked to "support the implementation of the defence and security measures of the Agreement [on Peace and Reconciliation in Mali] ... and to coordinate international efforts ... to rebuild the Malian security sector, within the framework set out by the Agreement".[135]

In our view, the list of peacekeeping missions encompassing SSR in their mandates includes two other missions – UNMIK (UN Mission in Kosovo) and UNAMID (African Union/UN Hybrid Mission in Darfur) – since their mandates refer to tasks that are related implicitly to one or more components of an SSR process. UNMIK has to provide an interim and transitional administration "while establishing and overseeing the development of provisional democratic self-governing institutions".[136] In addition, it is tasked to promote, organize and oversee the development of provisional democratic institutions and, pending a final settlement on the status of Kosovo, it is in charge of civil order, including establishing the local police.[137] Concerning UNAMID, its second strategic priority consists of mediating between the government of Sudan and armed groups based on the Doha Document for Peace in Darfur,[138] and the mission is encouraged to "engage fully in support of the implementation" of this document,[139] which includes measures for the reform of the justice and military institutions.[140]

Table 2: UN peacekeeping missions[141]

	Chapter VI UN Charter	Chapter VII UN Charter	SSR explicit	SSR implicit	Mine action explicit	Mine action implicit	SSR and mine action
MINUSCA UN Multidimensional Integrated Stabilization Mission in the Central African Republic	–	X	X	–	–	X	X
MINUSMA UN Multidimensional Integrated Stabilization Mission in Mali	–	X	X	–	X	–	X
MINUSTAH UN Stabilization Mission in Haiti	–	X	X	–	–	–	–
MONUSCO UN Organization Stabilization Mission in the DRC	–	X	X	–	X	–	X
UNAMID AU/UN Hybrid Operation in Darfur	–	X	–	X	X	–	X
UNMIK UN Mission in Kosovo	–	X	–	X	X	–	X
UNISFA UN Interim Security Force for Abyei	–	X	–	–	X[142]	–	–
UNMIL UN Mission in Liberia	–	X	X	–	–	X	X
UNMISS UN Mission in the Republic of South Sudan	–	X	–	–	X[143]	–	–
UNOCI UN Operation in Côte d'Ivoire	–	X	X	–	–	X	X
MINURSO UN Mission for the Referendum in Western Sahara	X	–	–	–	X[144]	–	–
UNDOF UN Disengagement Observer Force	X	–	–	–	–	–	–
UNFICYP UN Peacekeeping Force in Cyprus	X	–	–	–	–	–	–
UNIFIL UN Interim Force in Lebanon	X	–	–	–	–	X[145]	–
UNMOGIP UN Military Observer Group in India and Pakistan	X	–	–	–	–	–	–
UNTSO UN Truce Supervision Organization	X	–	–	–	–	–	–
Total	6	10	6	2	7	4	7

Among these eight peacekeeping missions, seven do also have tasks in mine action. Four of them (MINUSMA, MONUSCO, UNAMID and UNMIK) have in their mandates tasks related to core mine action activities. Three other missions can be considered as implicitly related to mine action (MINUSCA, UNMIL and UNOCI) because they support mine action actors in achieving their objectives and/or encompass activities in PSSM.

- MINUSMA's mandate refers to mine action under the task of protection of civilians, and has to "assist the Malian authorities with the removal and destruction of mines and other explosive devices and weapons and ammunition management".[146]
- MONUSCO is tasked to "mitigate the risk to civilians before, during and after any military operation".[147] These risks include ERW, and UNMAS provides MRE, risk assessment and clearance. In addition, UNMAS provides support to stabilization by building capacities of national institutions to deal with contamination, collecting and destroying weapons during the DDR process and providing support to overall SALW management. Finally, in relation to the Peace, Security and Cooperation Framework, UNMAS supports national ownership by establishing weapons and ammunition depots and training security personnel in safe management.[148]
- UNAMID integrates mine action under the task of protection of civilians and facilitates the delivery of humanitarian assistance, which constitutes the mission's second strategic priority. The threat to civilians posed by unexploded ordnance is an indicator of this strategic priority.[149]
- UNMIK's mandate includes the task of "supervising demining until the international presence can, as appropriate, take over responsibility".[150]
- MINUSCA has to "seize and collect arms and any related material the transfer of which into the CAR [Central African Republic] violates the measures imposed by paragraph 54 of resolution 2127 and to record and dispose of such arms and related materiel as appropriate".[151] The mandate also calls on national and international stakeholders to coordinate with MINUSCA in ensuring "safe and effective management, storage and security of stockpiles of small arms and light weapons, and the collection and/or destruction of surplus, seized, unmarked, or illicitly held weapons and ammunition", and "further stresses the importance of incorporating such elements into SSR and DDR programmes".[152]
- UNMIL is mandated to collect and destroy arms and ammunition within the DDR programme.[153] This task is part of the support provided to the implementation of the ceasefire agreement, and includes the establishment of security conditions for humanitarian assistance.

- Finally, UNOCI's mandate requests the mission to assist the government of Côte d'Ivoire in "collecting and storing arms and registering all relevant information related to those arms".[154] To fulfil this task, the mandate calls on the government to give the mission access to stores of "all weapons, ammunition and related materiel of all armed security forces".[155] This request is related to the effective management of arms and ammunition, which plays an important role in the stabilization of the country in conjunction with SSR and DDR.[156] Mine action involvement in these activities is confirmed by UNMAS, which provides assistance to UNOCI in the field of protection of civilians, DDR and the reform of the country's security institutions.[157]

The review of peacekeeping missions' mandates shows that mine action and SSR are regularly related to the protection of civilians, establishment of a secure environment for delivering humanitarian assistance and DDR.[158] It also confirms the increasing importance of PSSM in relation to DDR processes. Of particular interest is MINUSCA's mandate, because it clearly emphasizes the need to connect PSSM with the SSR programme – a connection we also find in MONUSCO and UNOCI, and which testifies to a growing awareness of the need to address PSSM as a governance issue.

However, we are of the opinion that linkages remain limited between SSR and mine action for three reasons. First, mine action is mostly included in the mandates under the task of protection of civilians and providing a secure environment for delivering humanitarian assistance, and there is no significant linkage with the establishment of mine action institutions, which is a governance issue and is related to effectiveness and accountability. Second, mine action and SSR are mainly connected through PSSM activities and do not include some core mine action activities (MRE and victim assistance). Third, the linkage through human rights issues, which are related to mine action through the conventions, is absent despite the fact that they potentially support the promotion of justice and accountability. The general impression is that SSR and mine action are rather conducted in parallel, and there is no use of the entire spectrum of possible joint activities.

The assessment of the linkages between SSR and mine action requires looking at political/peacebuilding missions, which have expanded since the end of the Cold War. There are nine political/peacebuilding missions, and six have in their mandates activities explicitly or implicitly related to SSR. Of these six missions, three (UNAMA, UNSOM and UNSMIL) have in their mandates an explicit or implicit task in mine action.

Table 3: UN special political/peacebuilding missions[159]

	Chapter VI UN Charter	Chapter VII UN Charter	SSR explicit	SSR implicit	Mine action explicit	Mine action implicit	SSR and mine action
UNAMA UN Assistance Mission in Afghanistan	–	–	X	–	–	X[160]	X
UNAMI UN Assistance Mission for Iraq	–	–	–	X[161]	–	–	–
UNIOGBIS UN Integrated Peace-building Office in Guinea–Bissau	–	–	X	–	–	–	–
UNOCA UN Regional Office for Central Africa	–	–	–	–	–	–	–
UNOWA UN Office of the Special Representative of the Secretary –General for West Africa	–	–	X	–	–	–	–
UNRCCA UN Regional Centre for Preventive Diplomacy for Central Asia	–	–	–	–	–	–	–
UNSCOL Office of the UN Special Coordinator for Lebanon	–	–	–	–	–	–	–
UNSMIL UN Support Mission in Libya	–	X	–	X[162]	X	–	X
UNSOM UN Assistance Mission in Somalia	–	X[163]	X	–	X	–	X
Total	0	2	4	2	2	1	3

- UNAMA is mandated to support the Afghan government in taking full "leadership and ownership in security governance".[164] Concerning mine action, the mission's role is expressed through the monitoring and coordination of activities in the protection of civilians and the coordination of all UN agencies and programmes, including those supporting mine action.[165]

- UNSOM is tasked to support the federal government of Somalia and the African Union Mission in Somalia with strategic policy advice on "security sector reform, rule of law (including police, justice and corrections within the framework of the United Nations Global Focal Point), disengagement of combatants, disarmament, demobilization and reintegration, maritime security and mine action".[166]

- UNSMIL provides "support to key Libyan institutions"[167] and continues its efforts in defence and police by "engaging national security forces and armed groups to encourage their participation in the dialogue process, and in ongoing preparatory work on new security arrangements".[168] UNSMIL also "continues to convene regular international coordination meetings on Libyan defence sector reform in Tunis".[169] In mine action, UNSMIL contributes to "securing uncontrolled arms and related material and countering its proliferation"[170] and implements measures of Resolution 2144 (2014), including to control "arms and related materiel in Libya and counter their proliferation, by working to arrange access, ensure proper management, safe storage and, where appropriate, effective disposal of arms and related materiel, [and] to support coherent partner effort in this regard, including coordination and facilitation of international assistance".[171]

These figures confirm the important role that SSR plays in peacebuilding and its political nature. Concerning mine action, missions' tasks are focused on protection of civilians and control, storage and disposal of arms and ammunition, and promoting a broader view of mine action by including activities such as PSSM. However, as for the peacekeeping missions, political/peacebuilding missions provide a limited linkage between SSR and mine action.

Overall, out of 25 peacekeeping and political/peacebuilding missions, ten have SSR and mine action in their mandates, but SSR and mine action seem to be conducted in parallel and follow a "division of labour" instead of operating jointly. The overlap occurs mainly in relation to PSSM, as shown by the mandates of MINUSCA, MONUSCO, UNOCI and UNSMIL. These missions seem to be the only ones suggesting a stronger connection between SSR and mine action to promote stabilization of the country. MINUSCA's mandate speaks directly of "incorporating" PSSM in SSR; MONUSCO relies on UNMAS for support in capacity building that should help stabilization and national ownership; and finally UNSOM is tasked to provide "strategic advice" in both SSR and mine action.

This paper does not propose that mine action should be merged with SSR. Nevertheless, we are of the opinion that in the mandates the linkages are limited, as there is no indication of possible connections at the level of normative and governance dimensions. Ultimately, the mandates do not reflect the potential synergies that were identified in the previous sections and would be beneficial for both SSR and mine action[172] and the achievement of missions' goals.

In addition, a better use of potential synergies would support missions in addressing the challenges identified by the 2013 UN Secretary-General's report on SSR. This report says that despite the progress made, SSR still needs to go beyond a "pillar approach" and undertake "sector-wide interventions".[173] It also highlights that SSR faces the challenge of contributing to long-term security through reforms and at the same time to "immediate security delivery through, for example, community-oriented policing, justice delivery and small arms and light weapons control".[174] Finally, the report underscores that SSR needs "to be linked to a broader set of practice areas".[175]

In relation to these challenges, this paper argues that enhanced linkage with mine action can support SSR in dealing with the provision of security in both short and long terms. In the short term, mine action can strengthen SSR through not only PSSM but also all its core activities. In particular, the overlap between SSR and the five constitutive pillars of mine action[176] could be more strongly stated, especially for victim assistance and MRE, which reflect human security concerns.

In the long term, support to SSR is possible in two ways. First, mine action demands the development of institutions, policies and a legal framework for programmes dealing with mines, ERW and cluster munitions. In this regard, closer cooperation between SSR and mine action would contribute to effectiveness and accountability of the security sector and would be a step in preventing relapse into conflict.[177] Second, the pillars of victim assistance, MRE and advocacy are related to human rights and create a link with reconciliation and justice components. The relevance of these pillars is based on mine-action-related conventions that require States Parties to provide assistance to victims; on the Maputo Action Plan that demands integration of such assistance into the national legal frameworks;[178] and on the CCM that mentions the need for age- and gender-sensitive assistance.[179] Moreover, the three pillars promote the development of civil society and its role as an active actor in the oversight of the security sector. These three pillars rely on the involvement of civil society organizations for raising awareness on people's rights, assisting mine victims, conducting training in risk education and building support for the conventions. Ultimately, the pillars have the potential to contribute to SSR by supporting local ownership and accountability and improving effectiveness by addressing people's security concerns.

National ownership and capacity development

As seen in the second section, national ownership is a central principle in mine action and has been referred to as "a cornerstone" of the APMBC and IMAS.[180]

Increasing numbers of countries affected by mines and ERW are approaching completion[181] of identifying and clearing all known contaminated areas, thereby transitioning from a phase of predominantly proactive survey and clearance activities to one of reactive response to reported threats. This transition means that concepts related to national capacity development and national ownership become more central, as there is a greater focus on sustainable national capacities to manage residual contamination,[182] rather than relying on internationally funded operators to carry out the work. The transition to a reactive approach also means that mine action capacities may be reduced in size and integrated in broader security structures such as the military or the police, thus interaction will increase in the future between mine action and security providers which may not have been involved during the proactive phase of mine action.

A limited number of mine-affected countries have enjoyed full national ownership of their mine action programmes from the very onset of survey and clearance activities. Nicaragua is a rare example of this: the Nicaraguan army cleared all minefields while benefiting from support from the Organization of American States (OAS). In most countries, however, it is predominantly international mine action organizations that implement proactive survey and clearance activities, with marginal or no involvement of national operators and national police and army. In several cases UNMAS and UNDP coordinate mine action programmes on behalf of affected countries. This underlines the importance of developing national capacities and ownership.

An example of successful capacity development and collaboration between SSR and mine action can be found in Liberia, illustrating how UNMAS implemented capacity development training with the national security providers and, with its implementing partner, collaborated effectively with several SSR stakeholders.

The Armed Forces of Liberia (AFL) and Liberia National Police (LNP) committed serious crimes against the civilian population during the 14-year civil war, resulting in little trust in the national security services. Recognizing this, key stakeholders in the Comprehensive Peace Accord process acknowledged the importance of reforming the security sector by including SSR in the August 2003 agreement.

As a result, UNMIL was established in September 2003 with a number of tasks related to SSR, including assisting Liberia's transitional government in monitoring and restructuring the LNP and forming a new and restructured AFL. Furthermore, UNMIL was responsible for responding to hazardous threats and carrying out explosive ordnance disposal (EOD)[183] of residual contamination. The transition plan outlining the transfer of responsibilities from UNMIL to the Liberian government foresaw that, by 2015, UNMIL's military capacity would be reduced to one engineering unit with EOD capacity, and that EOD responsibilities should be handed over to the AFL that same year.[184]

Given the gradual reduction of UNMIL troops and the resulting decline in EOD capacity, a 2011 internal UNMIL gap assessment identified the need to develop national EOD capacity. On this basis, UNMIL requested UNMAS to support transitioning the EOD response from UNMIL to national security services. UNMAS established a project in mid-2013 with the objective of training 32 AFL members as EOD operators.[185]

While significant training targeting the AFL had been under way in Liberia for several years, it was only when UNMAS established its presence there in 2013 that activities related to national clearance capacity development truly started. After successfully completing the training, AFL personnel carried out one EOD task in 2013 and nine in the first four months of 2014, a clear indication of the AFL's strengthened capacity to respond to and address residual contamination.[186]

Stockpiles of conventional weapons such as mines and cluster munitions have traditionally been the responsibility of the armed forces. Stockpile destruction is therefore another thematic area where SSR and mine action interact on the ground, and several examples illustrate how mine action organizations work with national armies in such processes. The engagement of Norwegian People's Aid (NPA), one of the biggest mine action operators globally, is a prominent example in this context and warrants closer analysis. NPA has developed the Self-Help Ammunition Destruction Options Worldwide (SHADOW) programme that seeks to assist states with the timely destruction of their cluster munition stockpiles. The programme responds to a clear need to identify safe, practical and cost-effective solutions for local and national small-scale cluster munition stockpile destruction. The first national self-help project was undertaken in Moldova in 2010, designed by NPA and the Moldovan Ministry of Defence (MOD). While the demolition stage of the process was entirely controlled by and the responsibility of the MOD and the national army, NPA developed capacities and provided supervision to army personnel for the disassembly stage of the destruction process.[187] The implementation phase resulted in the destruction of Moldova's cluster bomb stockpiles in just 17 days.[188] As of November 2014, NPA had implemented SHADOW projects in Croatia, Macedonia, Mozambique and Serbia and is planning activities in additional countries.

NPA notes that national ownership is a precondition for the successful implementation of SHADOW activities, as they depend on close collaboration and coordination with senior representatives of national governments and security providers.[189] NPA emphasizes that it is critical to secure high-level political commitment at the national level, and to identify "national champions" on which the organization can rely. NPA believes that its notable involvement in the CCM at the international political level has facilitated its strong relationships with several CCM States Parties. These have in turn been instrumental for the successful implementation of SHADOW.

Interestingly, and perhaps contrary to expectations, NPA has not experienced any particular challenges during its interactions with national militaries in implementation of activities, and points out that working closely with these militaries has been a very positive experience.[190] The fact that NPA receives SHADOW-related requests from the highest government levels, including from senior representatives of ministries of defence and foreign affairs, means that a high-level commitment is secured from the outset.

The SHADOW programme is an interesting example of an international mine action NGO providing capacity development support to national security services, thereby strengthening national ownership of the destruction process while contributing to fulfilling obligations under international law.

Good governance: Transparency, accountability and effectiveness

As seen in the previous sections, mine action conventions and IMAS create a solid international framework composed of both legal and non-legal norms. There is thus significant potential for joint work between SSR and mine action based on their shared commitment to the principles of good governance. In particular, better links between these two communities of practice would, on the one hand, improve transparency, accountability and effectiveness of mine action institutions and programmes; on the other hand, they would make SSR more comprehensive by better including mine action, which has the potential to be more than a related process, as indicated in the standard representation of SSR (illustrated in Figure 1), because in some post-conflict contexts it can actually be one of the most relevant security issues.

Despite this potential for synergies, SSR and mine action programmes do not interact significantly on good governance issues. While some examples from the field illustrate the interest in nurturing interlinkages between SSR and mine action, they equally show that there is currently limited cooperation among these two communities of practice.

Nepal is a case in point to underscore that the effectiveness of mine action is at some point undermined by the lack of a proper institutional set-up ensuring transparency and civilian oversight. This is well documented in a study by the Geneva International Centre for Humanitarian Demining (GICHD)[191] that analyses the achievements and challenges in establishing mine action institutions in the aftermath of the civil war. The study notes that despite the important accomplishment of freeing the country from the threat of mines and developing capacity for addressing the remaining threat from IEDs, mine action in Nepal has had some limitations.

In particular, the analysis points out that Nepal lacks "the institutional architecture for a national mine action programme under civilian coordination and oversight".[192] The Ministry of Peace and Reconstruction was supposed to become the civilian centre for coordination and oversight of national programmes, but failed to assume this role because it lacked the capacities in information and quality management. In addition, the Mine Action Steering Committee did not adopt a national mine action strategy, failed to develop national standards and guidelines, and became as ineffective as the Mine Action Joint Working Group – a body responsible for coordination between civilian and security actors in mine action.[193]

Due to the lack of civilian institutions, mine action has remained essentially in the hands of the Nepal Army (NA), and this is not without consequences. The NA Mine Action Coordination Centre (NAMACC) has retained the capacity to use the Information Management System for Mine Action (IMSMA),[194] but data on victims are not included because the NA maintains that it does not have any mandate for tracking victims. Data on victims have instead been kept by the human rights NGO Informal Sector Service,[195] which does not have IMSMA capacity. Therefore, data on mines and mine-related incidents entered into IMSMA are neither comprehensive nor complete.

In addition, information requests about mine incidents have to be addressed to NAMACC and must follow military channels, which is an obstacle for demands from civilian organizations. According to the authors of the study, only a new constitution and a significant SSR process would create the necessary space for a reconfiguration of the institutional responsibilities in mine action.[196]

The example of Nepal provides a number of lessons. First, it demonstrates that the broader governance of the security sector has an important influence on the overall management of mine action. In fact, the NA control over mine action is related to the incompleteness of the reforms included in the peace agreements.[197] Second, the lack of civilian leadership undermines not only mine action accountability but also its effectiveness, as information sharing is weakened. Consequently, SSR is seen as a key process for improving mine action institutions and programmes.

The importance of the governance dimension is also demonstrated by the case of Ukraine, which is confronted with a contamination problem from past conflicts, excessive stockpiles from the Soviet era and new contamination from mines and unexploded ordnance due to the crisis in its eastern and southeastern regions.[198]

In Ukraine there is no single body in charge of mine action at the time of writing and responsibilities are distributed among a number of institutions. The main institution is the State Emergency Service (SES), which is currently under the Ministry of Interior[199] but in the past it was a ministry in itself. Alongside the SES, there is the MOD with the armed forces' engineer corps, border guards and the Ministry of Infrastructure with its Special Transportation Service in charge of clearing transport infrastructure such as railways and highways. This situation creates important challenges in terms of coordination, duplication of capacities and lack of clarity about responsibilities for clearance.[200]

The Ukrainian state is aware of these challenges, and has started drafting a mine action law to establish a single body responsible for mine action. This process is complicated by the current conflict, which makes it difficult to separate humanitarian from military demining activities clearly. A presidential decree has assigned mine action activities to the MOD,[201] and the MOD is reluctant to relinquish its responsibilities to a civilian body as some activities related to mine action are perceived to be a matter of national security. Particularly sensitive are the sharing of information and access to areas close to the front lines.

Ukraine has received assistance in dealing with mines in the past, and the current conflict has increased the international presence in both SSR and mine action. The European Union Advisory Mission for Civilian Security Sector Reform was established in July 2014 with a mandate to provide advisory, mentoring and support services to law enforcement agencies (police, border guards, national guard, penitentiary and security service), the judiciary and public prosecution, and also includes cross-cutting aspects like anti-corruption, human rights, public administration reform and strategic communication.[202] In June 2015 the UN Mine Action Sub-Cluster was established under the chair of UNDP and the Danish Demining Group (DDG), and gathers state authorities and international actors working in mine action.[203] DDG is active in MRE, surveys and building demining capacities.[204] The Swiss Foundation for Mine Action and the International Trust Fund for Human Security are also active in MRE.[205] In addition, the Organization for Security and Co-operation in Europe Project Co-ordinator in Ukraine (OSCE PCU) has been in the country since 1999 and has helped Ukraine in enhancing its security, legislation, institutions and practices according to democratic standards to build "a secure environment for its people".[206] In mine action specifically, the OSCE PCU has supported the Ukrainian SES in developing its capacities.[207] NATO has been active in support of the destruction of landmines, SALW, ammunition and human-portable air-defence systems through its Trust Fund.[208]

Despite the significance of this international presence, there is limited interaction between SSR and mine action with few exceptions. The sub-cluster members provided comments on the draft law in July 2015.[209] The GICHD, in partnership with the OSCE PCU and the Geneva Centre for the Democratic Control of Armed Forces (DCAF), organized a conference to support Ukraine in the establishment of mine action institutions and continues to provide assistance on this matter.[210] This activity has proven the relevance of good governance in mine action, because the establishment of a single effective, accountable and civilian agency in mine action would produce several benefits including the capacity to:

- address issues of information gathering and sharing on contamination;
- build local capacities;
- facilitate coordination with international stakeholders;
- facilitate fundraising.

However, this GICHD, DCAF and OSCE PCU initiative is an isolated case and faces the challenges of bridging communities that usually do not interact. Mine action actors are more focused on operational matters such as the delivery of MRE and marking and clearing land, and tend to leave institutional development to other actors. Overall, the Ukraine case confirms that the mine action community of practice has margin to enhance its engagement in good governance issues, and SSR can provide valuable assistance to mine action by introducing a more political- and conflict-sensitive analysis.

People-centred approach and human rights

Not many concrete examples were found where SSR and mine action contribute jointly – directly or indirectly – to the protection and promotion of human rights. But one case in point relates to efforts undertaken in the CAR since 2014 under the umbrella of MINUSCA, of which UNMAS, human rights and SSR are components.

The history of violations of IHL and human rights in the CAR is tragically rich, involving both security forces and armed groups. The need for SSR goes far back, but in the aftermath of elections in 2005, when General Bozizé was elected two years after seizing power, violence took on a new momentum with the political and security dysfunctions of the state continuing to threaten stability and legitimacy. Armed groups challenged state power, and regular forces – including the Forces armées centrafricaines (FACA) – carried out security-sapping activities, including gross human rights abuses. It was also the time when the need to start thinking about the structural causes of conflict, including the set-up and functioning of the entire security system, was increasingly recognized. In 2008 SSR efforts to reform the FACA and other security providers began. These attempts largely failed before, but also in light of, the resumption of large-scale violence in 2012.[211]

In late 2012 violence resumed between the mainly Muslim Séléka rebel coalition and the government, and did not cease despite the 2013 Libreville peace agreement between the Bozizé government and the rebels. After the ousting of President Bozizé by the Séléka in March 2013, a transitional government took office. Conflict became more and more sectarian between the Séléka and the mainly Christian anti-Balaka movement, which led the UN Secretary-General to warn of the risk of a sectarian partition of the CAR.[212] Across the country security deteriorated, leading to weak government authority and control over national territory, human right abuses with total impunity and a severe humanitarian and protection crisis, with civilians being targeted by all armed groups. Security forces have contributed to general insecurity and committed numerous human rights violations against civilians.[213] Under these circumstances, the UN Security Council took action by establishing MINUSCA in March 2014.

Accountability and justice measures are recognized as essential in any peace and reconciliation process and to prevent ongoing violations in the short term.[214] Thus in the mandate of MINUSCA the Security Council stressed the need to end impunity and bring to justice perpetrators of violations and abuses – hence the critical role of SSR, specifically recognized by the Security Council[215] – and to disarm, demobilize, reintegrate and repatriate (DDRR) former combatants and armed elements. This imperative also applies to security forces, which, as described above, have a record of human rights abuses. As a consequence, MINUSCA supports SSR processes.[216] Vetting for human rights and other abuses has become a precondition for integration into the army.[217]

Similarly, the Security Council mandated MINUSCA to support the transitional authorities to "address the illicit transfer, destabilizing accumulation, and misuse of small arms and light weapons in the CAR, and to ensure the safe and effective management, storage and security of stockpiles of small arms and light weapons".[218] Surplus, seized, unmarked or illicitly held weapons and ammunition should also be collected and destroyed. UNMAS, being the UN focal point for mine action, assumes these responsibilities.

The deteriorated security situation has in fact facilitated the circulation of large quantities of weapons, obsolete ammunition and small arms ammunition. The UN recorded that 83 per cent of the obsolete ammunition and explosive remnants and 99 per cent of ammunition holdings had disappeared from inspected stockpiles between December 2012 and November 2013.[219] Related to these humanitarian and security risks, and at the same time contributing to them, large quantities of ammunition are poorly stored and managed.

On this basis UNMAS supports PSSM, which in the CAR implies the construction of safe and secured armouries and ammunition depots.[220] As a concrete example, on 27 April 2015 MINUSCA, through UNMAS and under the guidance of SSR, initiated the construction of a permanent armoury in Camp Kassaï with the capacity to store 1,000 weapons.[221] The armoury will help the transitional authorities to control the illicit transfer of arms better while ensuring their marking and safe management.[222] This effort is part of the strategy to reconstruct the armed forces.

The Security Council clearly stressed that these weapons-related activities should be incorporated into SSR and DDR/DDRR programmes.[223] The call for integration rests on the wider recognition of the links between national SALW management, reduction of armed violence, human rights issues and SSR.[224] The support provided by UNMAS to the transitional government in the CAR is a case in point of how these interlinkages can be effectively implemented. The respective activities of UNMAS and the SSR and human rights units of the mission are coordinated under the pillar of the political Deputy Special Representative of the Secretary-General; while UNMAS is mandated to support weapons and ammunition management, the SSR unit addresses structural and governance challenges.

Human rights violations and abuses are a major concern in the CAR, and the need for bold action against impunity and in vetting security sector personnel is significant. Furthermore, in accordance with its human rights due diligence policy, the UN is obliged to withdraw support from security actors who commit human rights violations or fail to address them.[225] The issue of constructing armouries might possibly be wisely used to leverage increased focus by the transitional government on human rights due diligence within its security sector. Such commitment, as well as the safety of storage sites, might also be considered under certain circumstances as among the prerequisites for the return of collected weapons to the transitional government. In his statement on the occasion of the opening of the construction site at Camp Kassaï, Under-Secretary-General Hervé Ladsous at least finely alluded to this when praising in this context the initiatives of the MOD and the general staff to develop an operational army that is irreproachable and responding increasingly to international norms.[226]

While this remark might seem anecdotal, it perfectly illustrates the interplay between broader mine action and SSR on the ground, and how the operationalization of such linkages can inform and contribute indirectly to the promotion of human rights. It is argued that such successful cross-fertilization among domains has the potential to be more widely explored when the specific political and operational circumstances on the ground allow.

As for human rights, research has shown that while each domain focuses extensively on integrating and mainstreaming gender and diversity in its respective operations, concrete joint projects are missing. The question therefore arises of whether stronger cooperation on this matter is relevant on the ground. As demonstrated conceptually, gender and diversity are cross-cutting issues with importance for both SSR and mine action, particularly in relation to institutions, recruitment, planning and delivery of support. Only when being inclusive can SSR and mine action be effective and achieve the greatest impact. Collecting and analysing gender-disaggregated data also represent important tasks of both SSR and mine action projects on the ground.

The common interest in the topic and the benefits from synergies of cooperation have started to be recognized, at least at headquarters level, as testified by an initiative of several Geneva-based organizations active in peace and security. In January 2015 a collaboration between DCAF, the Geneva Centre for Security Policy, the GICHD, Small Arms Survey and the Gender and Mine Action Programme, which are all housed at the Maison de la paix premises, resulted in the establishment of the Maison de la paix Gender and Diversity Hub. The strength of this initiative consists in bringing together under one umbrella the gender and diversity expertise of each organization in its specific thematic field and capitalizing on the resulting synergies, increased outreach and impact.

Given that promoting gender equality and diversity are integral both to SSR and mine action (and to other related fields such as SALW and security policy) and that, in some instances, both domains work with the same or similar stakeholders, it can be reasonably argued that joint delivery of gender and diversity support and advice lead to increased understanding of the gender- and diversity-related linkages for broader security and improved SSR and mine action programmes. The activities of the Gender and Diversity Hub will provide an opportunity to assess whether this assumption holds true.

Broadening mandates: Mine action organizations and security providers

After reviewing the operationalization – or lack thereof – of conceptual commonalities between SSR and mine action, this subsection adds a further analytical layer to the linkages between the SSR and mine action communities by examining how the trend for mine action organizations to broaden their activities has led to increased interaction with the security sector and whether this interaction has already or may in future yield synergies.

This trend is driven by the recognition that, in some contexts, expertise and capacities of mine action organizations are relevant and applicable to respond to needs in fields of activities beyond core mine action.[227] Interaction with these other domains brings the potential to contribute significantly to a response which is more efficient, better targeted and has greater impact. Another factor that has prompted mine action organizations to broaden their support is their proven ability to work in unstable and conflict-affected contexts. This type of expertise has enabled them to work in environments of multiple risks where SALW, IEDs and ammunition often pose additional and mutually reinforcing threats.

Other key factors are normative and diplomatic developments in recent years on SALW control, ammunition management and linking armed violence and development. Examples include the Arms Trade Treaty, the UN Programme of Action on SALW control,[228] regional agreements such as the 2006 Economic

Community of West African States Convention on Small Arms and Light Weapons, Their Ammunition and Other Related Materials, the IATG, ISACS and the Geneva Declaration on Armed Violence and Development. These instruments have provided mine action organizations with an important framework to assess and offer, where applicable, broader assistance to states. Requests for support have often been facilitated by the relationships established and trust developed between states and organizations during traditional mine action operations.

The following paragraphs highlight a series of cases in which previously traditional mine action organizations have started to address broader threats to security: the OAS SALW and ammunition destruction programme in Guatemala, DDG's Community Safety Programme in Uganda, a PSSM project undertaken by UNMAS and HALO Trust in Côte d'Ivoire and HALO Trust's involvement in DDR in Afghanistan. These projects were selected for their strong interaction with security forces and SSR processes.

Firstly, the broadening of their fields of activities led mine action organizations to deal with the destruction of SALW and ammunition, exemplified by OAS engagement in Guatemala. In that country more than 200,000 people were killed and many more subjected to human rights violations during the 36-year internal armed conflict.[229] Since the 1996 peace accords donors have invested significant amounts of money in security and justice reform, but with little result. Guatemala remains one of the most violent countries in the world, with a homicide rate of 34 per 100,000 persons in 2013, twice the Latin American average.[230] The level of violence and prevailing sense of insecurity are exacerbated by a lack of police capacity and mistrust of government security forces in many sectors of Guatemalan society.[231] Guatemala has also become a regional hub for the trafficking of SALW and ammunition.

Following a fire in 2005 at a military ammunition storage depot containing highly volatile white phosphorus based within densely populated Guatemala City, the white phosphorus was stored in temporary bunkers. For five years no action was taken to address the underlying problem, and the phosphorus continued to deteriorate. This increasingly posed an environmental and security threat, along with the fear that other ammunition depots in urban areas were at risk of igniting. Thus the Guatemalan military identified the need to reduce the risk of unplanned explosions and improve its stockpile management capacity. Guatemala had significant stocks of ammunition resulting from obsolete weaponry and surpluses beyond national defence and security needs.[232]

In 2010, when the OAS was approached to assist with destroying the legacy of the 2005 accident, it started to support the safe removal and management of ammunition.[233] This support reflects an internal evolution within the OAS which culminated in the establishment of a dedicated programme of assistance for control of arms and ammunition, in addition to its traditional programme for comprehensive action against anti-personnel mines.

An initial survey in 2010 carried out by the OAS and its contractor Golden West, an expert humanitarian NGO, concluded that 600 tons required destruction, much of which consisted of excess, expired and obsolete ammunition.[234] With inadequate stockpile management, excess weapons and ammunition cannot be identified and pose a grave year-to-year risk.[235] However, Guatemala, like other countries in the region, lacked capacity, especially in the Ordnance Service of the Ministry of National Defence in charge of munitions storage facilities. In response to this need, the OAS assisted the military in identifying, transporting and eliminating both small- and large-calibre explosive ammunition located in military storage sites in densely populated areas, and delivered specialized training in destruction and demolition techniques. As a result of the project, Guatemala's problem of excess and obsolete ammunition has largely been addressed.[236]

In addition, the OAS started to be involved in SALW destruction. As previously mentioned, Guatemala has become a regional hub for SALW trafficking with significant levels of illicit arms in circulation. With training, technical and logistical assistance, and equipment provided by the OAS, the Guatemalan military has worked with the judicial authorities to destroy SALW that were seized. Finally, the Guatemalan military has also taken steps to destroy its own supplies of excess and obsolete SALW.[237]

This OAS project focusing on SALW and ammunition destruction has had an important impact on the physical security of ammunition storage sites and the availability of SALW. Furthermore, it has greatly contributed to enhancing the effectiveness of the security sector. Collaboration between the Guatemalan military and the OAS has enhanced the credibility of the military, and of the ammunition and SALW destruction process.[238]

Engaging with the agents of violence is another example of how mine action organizations broaden their mandate, illustrated by DDG's Community Safety Programme in Uganda. The Karamoja region suffers from high levels of conflict and insecurity and is one of the most marginalized in Uganda, with 82 per cent of the population living below the poverty line.[239] The region is characterized by protracted interclan conflicts over cattle, grazing land and access to other resources.

The Karamajong are semi-nomadic pastoralists who depend on cattle grazing and cattle raiding for their livelihoods. In the 1970s cattle herds were reduced by drought and disease, which led to increased raiding. The increased frequency of raids led to an increased demand for weapons, for both raiding and defending herds. With the growing proliferation of SALW since the 1970s, the lethality of interclan cattle raids has increased dramatically. A 2008 estimate indicated that with a small arms death rate of 600 per 100,000, Karamoja has the highest level of SALW-related deaths and injuries in Uganda.[240]

An assessment conducted by Saferworld revealed rampant abuse by security providers, lack of access to them, lack of information on their activities and lack of community consultation. Many residents complained that the police were not proactive in engaging communities, and people remained unaware of their rights.[241] In spite of their violent behaviour, communities consider the presence of the Uganda People's Defence Forces (UPDF) as necessary to provide security to farms and recover stolen livestock, but they maintain a better relationship with local councils and traditional elders.[242]

DDG was founded in the late 1990s, initially specializing in clearing landmines and unexploded ordnance, but has expanded its activities from traditional mine action to include broader initiatives aimed to prompt positive change in the agents as well as institutional and cultural environments of violence.[243] Active in Uganda through a mine/ERW clearance programme in association with the UPDF and the Uganda Police Force (UPF) since 2007, DDG decided to expand its operations by launching a programme to improve community safety in the conflict-prone Karamoja region. With its Community Safety Programme, DDG strives to create the preconditions for sustainable development by addressing the causes and impacts of instability, conflict and armed violence. It aims especially to develop the capacity of communities to mitigate conflict at all levels and the capacity of formal security providers to meet the security needs of communities.

The first phase of the project consists of in-depth consultations with key security providers, in particular the UPDF and UPF. Actual implementation commences upon permission from communities, with the establishment of community safety plans. These focus on clarifying participants' vision of community safety and developing an action plan. Community safety committees, including elders, women, youth, political leaders and security providers, are then responsible for implementing the action plans.[244]

Subsequently, conflict management education is delivered alongside efforts to strengthen existing formal and informal judicial systems to resolve conflict. Education takes place at village level with the participation of about 70–100 households. DDG is also delivering conflict management education for the police and UPDF. Education is complemented by SALW sensitization, which is a sensitive issue as SALW ownership is illegal in Uganda and also because government-sponsored forced disarmament campaigns, implemented by the UPDF, have involved extrajudicial executions and torture of the Karamajong.[245]

Finally, in response to past abuse and human rights violations by security forces, DDG facilitates regular meetings between community representatives and their main security providers. At the end of these meetings, resolutions are agreed and signed by all participants. Examples of issues discussed include the mistreatment of people by the UPF and UPDF, rapes by security providers and the wearing of traditional scarves by young warriors, which security forces believed were concealing SALW.[246]

DDG's Community Safety Programme has clearly had a significant positive impact. Regular meetings between communities and security providers contributed to reduced violence. What is more, in 2010 27.7 per cent of participating community members in five parishes stated that their trust in the police was very good. This figure increased to 41.1 per cent in 2011.[247] Slight improvements in the relationship between communities and the UPDF were also recorded. Security providers have noted that community members have become more open about reporting cases, and communities have stated that the security providers have become more sensitive when dealing with them.[248]

While some mine action organizations have addressed the agents of armed violence, as illustrated in DDG's Community Safety Programme, their broadening support mainly relates thus far to PSSM. This new field of activity is illustrated by a joint UNMAS–HALO Trust project in Côte d'Ivoire.

In 2002 Côte d'Ivoire started to endure conflict between the north, which was held by rebels, and the south, controlled by then President Laurent Gbabgo's forces. Violence rose significantly following the 2010 presidential elections, when intense fighting broke out between Gbabgo and election winner Ouattara. During these long years of conflict, armouries and ammunition depots were looted and damaged across the country and a significant amount of arms and ammunition got into civilian and militia hands. According to the Small Arms Survey, the number of illicit arms in circulation increased considerably during the crisis.[249]

Following the crisis, the UN received reports that mines had been laid along the line of confidence which divided the north and south of the country. The chief of the UNOCI DDR Division contacted UNMAS for assistance to confirm whether there was contamination. Beyond confirming unexploded ordnance and IED contamination, the initial assessment also highlighted a problem with abandoned ordnance, while noting that arms and ammunition in Republican Forces of Côte d'Ivoire (FRCI), gendarmerie and police depots and armouries had been looted. UNOCI DDR therefore asked UNMAS to increase ammunition storage safety.[250] As a result of UN Security Council Resolution 2000 (2011), UNMAS established a programme reporting to the DDR–SSR Division aiming to contribute to "protection and security", including via SALW collection and disposal, for the stabilization and reconstruction of the country.[251]

An institutional set-up was therefore put in place fostering close interaction between UNMAS and the SSR and DDR activities of UNOCI. This temporary[252] location of UNMAS under the DDR–SSR chapeau was considered helpful, especially to facilitate UNMAS access to security forces. Nonetheless, this example also sheds light on the need to create initial awareness and a shared understanding among the mine action, DDR and SSR communities after deployment to a mission.[253]

A national assessment of 56 police, gendarmerie and FRCI weapons and ammunition storage facilities between October 2011 and the end of June 2012 indicated that all sites would require significant improvements and that, if management practices were not enhanced, large-scale explosions could occur. The assessment revealed that in many cases ammunition was stored in buildings that were not originally designed as ammunition storage facilities and did not meet international standards.[254]

This assessment informed planning for the establishment of secure temporary stores and the rehabilitation and future management of the regular sites. Hence, among other activities, UNMAS supports UNOCI's SSR mandate by developing capacities of the national security forces to rehabilitate and refurbish their armouries and ammunition storage areas and developing their required technical expertise for efficient management of such sites.[255]

To achieve this objective, UNMAS contracted the NGO HALO Trust to implement a PSSM programme. Since then, HALO Trust and UNMAS have worked closely with the Ivorian authorities to build or renovate more than 190 stores and armouries and develop capacities of the security forces in safe weapons and ammunition management and destruction.[256]

While Côte d'Ivoire is another good example of capacity development, it also illustrates that support to address the threats of unsecured and/or inadequately managed stockpiles has created valuable synergies between UNMAS and SSR.[257] In 2013 UNOCI rightly pointed out that it would be of great importance to include PSSM in the drafting of the national defence policy.[258] Finally, it is a testimony to increased interaction between mine action organizations and broader security providers. In fact, the government of Côte d'Ivoire and the security forces, recognizing the risks posed by unsecured arms and ammunition, established a national PSSM working group which meets monthly and is chaired by the head of the FRCI Logistics Division. Beyond its purpose of exchanging good practice on PSSM, the group serves as a platform for planning and meeting training needs. UNMAS and HALO Trust are members of the group, as are representatives of the armed forces, gendarmerie and police.[259]

Before turning to interaction between SSR and mine action via DDR, it is worth noting that it is not a given that mine action organizations involved in PSSM are able to create linkages to SSR. A case in point is the experience of the NGO Mines Advisory Group (MAG) in Burundi. From 2007 to 2013 MAG worked with the Burundian police and army to develop their capacities to secure and manage their SALW stockpiles safely. MAG also trained army personnel to destroy surplus and obsolete weapons and ammunition.[260] By enhancing the capacity of armourers in the management of SALW and storage sites, MAG certainly contributed to the professionalization of the country's security and defence forces. It also made several attempts to link its PSSM support to wider SSR. However, it experienced challenges in engaging with SSR stakeholders on the ground. It appears that, at the time of MAG's PSSM project in Burundi, the wider SSR community considered that PSSM fell outside the scope of SSR.[261]

Securing financial support for MAG's PSSM project from SSR donors proved to be equally challenging. Especially the Netherlands has been very active in supporting SSR in Burundi, not least since the establishment of the Burundi–Netherlands Security Sector Development programme[262] in 2009. The programme has proven instrumental to build momentum towards greater transparency and accountability, and has been recognized as having the potential to lead effectively to governance results.[263] MAG was initially included in the first two-year block of programme projects with the Burundian police. However, funding for MAG's PSSM activities was discontinued, since the Netherlands no longer considered PSSM to be part of its wider SSR priorities. The weak link between PSSM and SSR was also articulated in Burundi's 2012–2015 strategic plan for SSR, in which PSSM figures only minimally.[264]

As a final example of the increasing involvement of mine action organizations in related fields of activity, the paper sheds light on the linkages between SSR and mine action on the ground through DDR. The success of SSR projects is often linked to effective demilitarization, and some authors argue that DDR and SSR should be planned, resourced, implemented and evaluated together.[265] As the following example mainly focuses on mine action organizations' efforts in the reintegration aspect of DDR, it is worth highlighting that successful reintegration directly contributes to the shared DDR–SSR objective of ensuring effective and sustainable transition of former combatants to civilian life. Failed reintegration can undermine SSR by putting pressure on police, courts and prisons, in addition to representing a security threat for the state and communities.[266]

Hence it seems logical that in Afghanistan DDR has been conceived as a pillar in SSR following the adoption of a peacebuilding and political transition roadmap – the Bonn Agreement – in late 2001.[267] In this context, Afghanistan's New Beginnings Programme used demining training as a way to reintegrate former combatants from the Afghan military forces into civilian life between 2004 and 2006. The steady income and benefits proved attractive to former combatants who were reintegrated into the workforce: 75 per cent were still working as deminers one month after the end of the programme, demonstrating an encouraging retention potential within mine action.[268]

In the subsequent Afghanistan Peace and Reintegration Programme (APRP), started in 2010, much weight was again put on reintegration, this time aimed at insurgents. Mine action's contribution to DDR falls within the third phase of reintegration, which is designed to demonstrate to communities the benefits of maintaining peace.[269]

The APRP refers reintegrees to participating demining agencies after they have been vetted, enrolled and provided with a stipend for transition assistance. By including both former insurgents and non-combatants, the APRP is careful not to "reward" those who participated in conflict or to exacerbate tensions within the community. Very importantly, reintegrees begin receiving a salary from day one of demining training, immediately relieving pressure to return to conflict for monetary reasons. In 2010 HALO Trust started to employ former combatants as deminers, and thus to support DDR explicitly. This initiative was based on HALO Trust's belief that by promoting peace and stability in its areas of operation, it would be able to perform its core activities better while at the same time contributing to broader peacebuilding goals. When reintegrees graduate from the training, they are assigned to demining teams that are deployed in the same way as all other HALO Trust teams.[270]

Many other APRP activities require a significant timespan to demonstrate results to both reintegrees and communities; in contrast, reintegration as deminers shows benefits from the first day of training. While demining has remained a small component of the overall APRP, it has proven to be an important and effective means of demonstrating the benefits of peace. Another added value of having reintegrated former combatants in teams alongside community deminers is that reconciliation is effectively nurtured. They learn to work together with former enemies towards a common goal. Deminers must be able to trust one another fully to work safely in the field.[271] HALO Trust has reintegrated hundreds of former Taliban and Hezbi Islami combatants in Baghlan and Kunduz provinces into its demining ranks and trained them as community-based deminers.[272]

Assisting directly in DDR initiatives can have repercussions for a neutral humanitarian organization such as HALO Trust. The employment of former combatants of an ongoing insurgency could be perceived by some as a partisan act siding with the government. While some assessments of HALO Trust's involvement in DDR in Afghanistan conclude that the NGO did not encounter any specific risks or threats as a result of the reintegration of former combatants,[273] others testify that its employees were perceived as spies and threatened.[274] Although the overall experience was seen as good, this clearly sheds light on the new challenges and risks for humanitarian NGOs when engaging in inherently political processes and working with former insurgents. As Blaney et al. pointed out, "DDR and SSR are political and dangerous efforts as they dismantle the de facto institutions of power in conflict-affected countries. A general or warlord may not welcome the suggestion to put down his gun and become a farmer. As such, purely technical approaches to DDR and SSR will fail."[275]

It is of course important for an NGO to mitigate these risks, for instance by underlining and communicating its neutral and technical work and its benefits for communities. Nevertheless, caution and close monitoring are required, since reputation and trust are much more easily lost than built.[276] Mine action organizations may also need to reinforce security measures for this very reason, since the risk of attacks against reintegrated fighters may increase.[277] In conclusion, the example of HALO Trust's involvement in DDR in Afghanistan illustrates the added value of mine action organizations' contribution to reforming the security sector.

In sum, it can be demonstrated that the common conceptual approaches of SSR and mine action are resulting in concrete linkages between both communities of practice in some areas, such as capacity development, national ownership and the promotion of human rights, while such linkages are largely missing in others, as in the case of gender and diversity. While this latter example might highlight room for new opportunities, it also raises the fundamental question as to the limits of potential synergies. Finally, the trend towards increased interaction between mine action organizations and security providers identified in this section might not necessarily be a given in all contexts.

Conclusion

This paper focuses on three questions aiming at identifying the linkages between SSR and mine action at conceptual and operational levels in post-conflict contexts. We show that both SSR and mine action share a common understanding of security: human security. This concept broadens the traditional state-centric definition of security and adopts a people-centred perspective which encompasses human safety, livelihood and dignity.

By focusing on national ownership, accountability and effectiveness, SSR aims to create conditions that are conducive not only to state and human security, but also to socio-economic development. Similarly, mine action actors have gone beyond the immediate removal of mines and ERW for humanitarian purposes and expanded their spectrum of activities to contribute to long-term development and address wider threats related to conventional weapons. Finally, this pattern of a broadening spectrum of activities and the recognition of the interdependencies of risks to state and human security match the qualitative change of UN peacekeeping and peacebuilding missions, which today fully integrate SSR and mine action where relevant.

The conceptual linkages between SSR and mine action are reflected by significant commonalities in their approach to designing and implementing programmes. This paper finds that both SSR and mine action programmes promote national ownership, give significant attention to the development of local capacities and seek to apply the principles of good governance. A people-centred, rights-based approach is at the core of SSR, not least because SSR mostly takes place in countries in which the security sector may have been a major threat to the human rights of its own constituency. A focus on people and human rights is also key in mine action, as it is anchored in international conventions addressing the humanitarian consequences of mines and ERW. Finally, both SSR and mine action mainstream gender equality and diversity, which are considered fundamental to ensuring effective, accountable and non-discriminatory provision of security.

Both domains have become components in UN peacekeeping and peacebuilding missions. MINUSCA and UNOCI are good examples testifying to the synergies from cooperation between SSR and mine action, with its increasingly related domains such as PSSM and SALW. MINUSCA has a mandate to incorporate PSSM into SSR and develop capacities in managing SALW. Connecting these activities may contribute indirectly to the promotion of human rights. UNOCI also gives PSSM an important role in the stabilization of the country. In addition to these cases, the paper demonstrates that the broadening involvement of mine action actors in related fields of activities has led them to work increasingly with DDR and security actors that are traditional stakeholders in SSR programmes. As illustrated by several examples, mine action can facilitate SSR by contributing to the professionalization of national security and defence forces, and consequently support capacity development and ownership.

Despite these positive trends, this paper also notes that interaction between SSR and mine action is still limited at field level. The synergies between them are mostly confined to PSSM and do not take advantage of the full spectrum of potential activities (mine action's five pillars) that could be conducted jointly to improve the impact of interventions on the ground. In particular, the paper identifies some areas in which opportunities for cooperation remain to be explored.

A potential area of cooperation is promotion of good governance. The example of Ukraine, where efforts are being made to support the development of well-governed, efficient and accountable mine action institutions by combining SSR and assistance to mine action, is an illustration of possible synergies. Another area is gender and diversity, which is a shared approach and a priority of both domains. The recent establishment of the Maison de la paix Gender and Diversity Hub in Geneva might be a first and encouraging sign of increasingly joint work on this critical aspect.

We recognize that some important differences between SSR and mine action render synergies challenging and, consequently, may explain the limitations in linking SSR and mine action in post-conflict contexts. A particular challenge is to bridge the political dimension of SSR and the humanitarian origin of mine action. On the one hand, this paper recognizes that SSR addresses politically sensitive issues, especially in post-conflict contexts where state institutions are contested or weak and control over the security sector is key to political influence and governance. On the other hand, it stresses that mine action has grown as a humanitarian activity abiding by the principles of neutrality, impartiality and independence. This feature has pushed mine action away from sensitive political questions and reduced the room for cooperation with SSR.

Another challenge relates to the strong operational and technical focus of mine action, which has at least three consequences. First, it may relegate broader security and institutional issues to a second order of priority. Second, the technical nature of mine action can overshadow its contribution to security governance and, as demonstrated by the case of Burundi, SSR actors may simply not perceive it as relevant to SSR. Third, there is often a "time lapse" because mine action actors tend to be early on the ground and have their programmes and network already established when SSR actors come into play. This renders cooperation more difficult, requiring a readjustment of already ongoing mine action programmes.

However, these differences should not undermine strong opportunities for enhancing the interaction between SSR and mine action. These opportunities are important, since they facilitate the delivery of SSR and mine action support by combining expertise and experience. Building bridges and operationalizing the shared approaches and objectives will prove valuable to address security issues from a broader and more holistic perspective, leading to increased impact and effectiveness of interventions.

Human security could play an important role to bridge divides and strengthen the interaction between SSR and mine action. This concept provides a general framework in which the specific goals of SSR and mine action are understood as contributing to one single goal. The human security concept, with its people-centred approach and the relevance given to human rights, gender and diversity, is instrumental in strengthening the existing common features between SSR and mine action.

At a more practical level, the paper identifies specific areas where SSR and mine action could benefit from improved cooperation. Mine action could contribute to overcoming the challenges identified by the 2013 report of the UN Secretary-General on SSR.[278] In particular, it could help SSR in bridging short- and long-term security provision by dealing with immediate threats from mines and ERW, on the one hand, and addressing longer-term challenges through the development of local capacities and institutions on the other hand. In addition, mine action has a more codified legal-normative framework than does SSR and this could be used to leverage issues that are at the core of both mine action and SSR agendas. Finally, the need for establishing mine action institutions is a potential entry point for SSR programmes.

Moreover, stronger linkages to SSR would be beneficial for a better understanding of the broader political and security context in which mine action institutions need to be developed. In other words, SSR's holistic nature complements mine action by providing a wider analysis of security needs and capacities. As seen in the cases of Nepal and Ukraine, the development of mine action capacities (or lack thereof) and their effectiveness are determined by the overall institutional security framework. SSR actors could facilitate contact with other national security stakeholders that are not among the usual interlocutors for mine action organizations but play a role in establishing mine action programmes and institutions, such as members of parliament.

Stronger interaction with security providers and SSR more generally also seems to result naturally from recent trends in mine action. First, while many mine-affected countries complete their clearance targets or treaty obligations, residual contamination may remain to be addressed. Instead of dedicated mine action institutions, this task often requires appropriate response capacities streamlined into security providers such as the military or police. Second, as mine action organizations increasingly address issues such as PSSM or DDR, their primary interlocutors may no longer necessarily be humanitarian bodies, but security actors. Given the ramifications of such issues in aspects of national security, mine action organizations may need to pay more attention to political considerations in the future and, as a result, take SSR priorities increasingly into account.

Post-conflict contexts in particular tighten the relationship between SSR and mine action for multiple reasons. First, in these environments mines and ERW often constitute a severe threat to security and an impediment to development, and must be addressed not only in the immediate aftermath of conflict but also in the long term to support socio-economic development, access to social services and the fulfilment of civic and human rights. Second, mine action requires appropriate, effective and accountable institutions which SSR aims also to create. Finally, these institutions and programmes involve a plurality of actors, from state ministries and agencies to local and international civil society, NGOs and corporations. Thus mine action has to address and solve issues and challenges that are common to all the other pillars of the security sector. Ultimately, the linkages between mine action and SSR demonstrate the importance of better articulating the close and sometimes cross-cutting relationship between these two agendas in order to improve the theory, policy and practice of post-conflict peacebuilding.

Notes

1   United Nations, *United Nations Peacekeeping Operations. Principles and Guidelines* (New York: United Nations, 2008), p. 26.

2   Oxford Dictionary definition of synergy: "The interaction or cooperation of two or more organizations, substances, or other agents to produce a combined effect greater than the sum of their separate effects", www.oxforddictionaries.com/definition/english/synergy.

3   Heiner Hänggi, "Making sense of security sector governance", in Heiner Hänggi and Theodor H. Winkler (eds), *Challenges of Security Sector Governance* (Münster: LIT, 2003), p. 5.

4   Ibid.; Albrecht Schnabel, "The security-development discourse and the role of SSR as a development instrument", in Albrecht Schnabel and Vanessa Farr (eds), *Back to the Roots: Security Sector Reform and Development* (Münster: LIT, 2012), p. 31.

5   Lloyd Axworthy, "Towards a new multilateralism", in Maxwell A. Cameron, Robert J. Lawson and Brian W. Tomlin (eds), *To Walk Without Fear: The Global Movement to Ban Landmines* (Don Mills, ON: Oxford University Press, 1998), p. 451.

6   United Nations, "Securing states and societies: Strengthening the United Nations comprehensive support to security sector reform", report of the Secretary-General, 13 August 2013, UN Doc. A/67/970-S/2013/480.

7   Edward Newman, "The United Nations and human security", in Mary Martin and Taylor Owen (eds), *Routledge Handbook of Human Security* (London: Routledge, 2014), p. 226.

8   UN Development Programme, *Human Development Report* (Oxford: Oxford University Press, 1994).

9   Ibid., p. 24.

10   Hänggi, note 3 above, pp. 5–6.

11   Nicole Ball and Dylan Hendrickson, "Trends in security sector reform (SSR): Policy, practice and research", paper prepared for workshop on "New Directions in Security Sector Reform", Peace, Conflict and Development Programme Initiative, International Development Research Centre, Ottawa, 3–4 November 2005 (Ottawa: IDRC, 2006), p. 8.

12   For critics of a broad human security approach see for instance Keith Krause, *Towards a Practical Human Security Agenda* (Geneva: DCAF, 2007); S. Neil Macfarlane, "A useful concept that risks losing its political salience", *Security Dialogue*, Vol. 35, No. 3 (2004), pp. 368–369; Andrew Mack, "The concept of human security", in Michael Brzoska and Peter J. Croll (eds), *Promoting Security: But How and for Whom?* (Bonn: BICC, 2004), pp. 47–50.

13   Taylor Owen, "Human security – Conflict, critique and consensus: Colloquium remarks and a proposal for a threshold-based definition", *Security Dialogue*, Vol. 35, No. 3 (2004), p. 378.

14   UN General Assembly, "Follow-up to paragraph 143 on human security of the 2005 World Summit Outcome", 25 October 2012, UN Doc. A/RES/66/290.

15   Axworthy, note 5 above, p. 451.

16   Heiner Hänggi, "Security sector reform – Concepts and contexts", in International Center for Innovation, *Transformation and Excellence in Governance (INCITEGov) Transformation: A Security Sector Reform Reader* (Passig City: INCITEGov, 2012), pp. 12–13.

17   DCAF/ISSAT, *SSR in a Nutshell* (Geneva: DCAF/ISSAT, 2012), p. 11.

18   Hänggi, note 16 above, p. 26.

19   OECD-DAC, *Security System Reform and Governance* (Paris: OECD-DAC, 2005), p. 3.

20   United Nations, *The United Nations SSR Perspective. Sustainable Peace Through Justice and Security* (New York: United Nations, 2012), p. 2.

21   Laurie Nathan, *No Ownership, No Commitment: A Guide to Local Ownership of Security Sector Reform* (Birmingham: University of Birmingham, 2007), p. 4.

22   Dustin Sharp, "Security sector reform for human security: The role of international law and transitional justice in shaping more effective policy and practice", in Matthew Saul and James A. Sweeney (eds), *International Law and Post-Conflict Reconstruction Policy* (London: Routledge, 2015), pp. 166–185.

23   Christoph Bleiker and Marc Krupanski, "The rule of law and security sector reform: Conceptualising a complex relationship", DCAF SSR Paper No. 5, Geneva, 2012.

24   Alan Bryden and Heiner Hänggi (eds), *Reform and Reconstruction of the Security Sector* (Geneva: DCAF, 2004); DCAF, *Gender & Security Sector Reform Toolkit* (Geneva: DCAF, 2008).

25   Albrecht Schnabel and Hans Born, "Security sector reform: Narrowing the gap between theory and practice", DCAF SSR Paper No. 1, Geneva, 2011, p. 30.

26   Ibid., p. 21.

27   Hänggi, note 16 above, p. 37.

28   Schnabel and Born, note 25 above, pp. 33–44.

29   Hänggi, note 16 above, p. 32.

30   Kristin Valasek, "Cross-cutting issues in security sector reform training and education", ASSET Practice Note, 2013, http://asset-ssr.org/images/pdf_file/english/PracticeNote2_CrosscuttingIssues_DCAF.pdf; DCAF/ISSAT, note 17 above, p. 11.

31   UNMAS, "Glossary of mine action terms, definitions and abbreviations", IMAS 04.10, para 3.176, p. 24.

32   For ease of reading, in the following "mine-affected" includes contamination by cluster munitions and ERW, if applicable to a specific country.

33   A mine can be defined, in its simplest form, as a munition designed to be placed under, on or near the ground or other surface area and to be exploded by the presence, proximity or contact of a person or a vehicle. See GICHD, *A Guide to Mine Action* (Geneva: GICHD, 2014), p. 16.

34   ERW comprise unexploded ordnance and abandoned explosive ordnance. See ibid., p. 18.

35   UNMAS, note 31 above, IMAS 04.10, para 3.176, p. 24.

36   Cluster munitions can be defined, in their simplest form, as a conventional munition that is designed to disperse or release explosive submunitions, each weighing less than 20 kilograms, and includes those explosive submunitions. See GICHD, note 33 above, pp. 16–17.

37   Chris Horwood, "Humanitarian mine action: The first decade of a new sector in humanitarian aid", Relief and Rehabilitation Network/Overseas Development Institute Network Paper No. 32, London, 2000, pp. 10, 31–32.

38   United Nations, "Convention on Prohibitions or Restrictions on the Use of Certain Conventional Weapons Which May Be Deemed to Be Excessively Injurious or to Have Indiscriminate Effects", Geneva, 10 October 1980, UN Doc. A/CONF.95/15.

39   Jean-Marie Henckaerts and Louise Doswald-Beck, *Customary International Humanitarian Law. Vol. 1: Rules* (Cambridge: Cambridge University Press, 2005). See also Additional Protocol I to the Geneva Conventions, which contains these rules explicitly.

40   "Convention on the Prohibition of the Use, Stockpiling, Production and Transfer of Anti-Personnel Mines and on Their Destruction", Oslo, 18 September 1997. The Convention is also referred to as "Anti-Personnel Mine Ban Convention" (APMBC).

41   John Borrie, *Unacceptable Harm. A History of How the Treaty to Ban Cluster Munitions Was Won* (New York and Geneva: UNIDIR, 2009), pp. 138 and 314.

42   GICHD, note 33 above, p. 37.

43   Kristian Berg Harpviken and Jan Isaksen, *Reclaiming the Field of War: Mainstreaming Mine Action in Development* (Oslo and New York: PRIO/UNDP, 2004); GICHD, *Linking Mine Action and Development. Guidelines for Policy and Programme Development: States Affected by Mines/ERW* (Geneva: GICHD, 2009).

44   In this paper we consider the five pillars as being the core of mine action; other activities are defined as fields related to mine action.

45 Sharmala Naidoo, "Mission creep or responding to wider security needs? The evolving role of mine action organisations in armed violence reduction", *Stability: International Journal of Security & Development*, Vol. 2 No. 1 (2013), pp. 1–8.

46 UN Security Council, Resolution 2040, UN Doc. S/RES/2040 (2012).

47 Eric G. Berman and Pilar Reina, "Unplanned explosions at munitions sites: Concerns and consequences", *Journal of ERW and Mine Action*, Vol. 16, No. 2 (2012), p. 4.

48 Benjamin King (ed.), *Safer Stockpiles. Practitioners' Experiences with Physical Security and Stockpile Management (PSSM) Assistance Programmes* (Geneva: SAS, 2011), pp. 2–3.

49 United Nations, note 1 above, pp. 21–31.

50 UN Security Council, Resolution 1925 (2010), UN Doc. S/RES/1925 (2010); UN Security Council, Resolution 2098 (2013), UN Doc. S/RES/2098 (2013). See also Mateja Peter, "Between doctrine and practice: The UN peacekeeping dilemma", *Global Governance*, Vol. 21 (2015), pp. 351–370.

51 Oliver Ramsbothan, Tom Woodhouse and Hugh Miall, *Contemporary Conflict Resolution*, 3rd edn (Cambridge: Polity Press, 2011), p. 163.

52 United Nations, note 1 above, p. 26.

53 Ibid., p. 19.

54 United Nations, "An agenda for peace: Preventive diplomacy, peacemaking and peace-keeping", report of the Secretary-General pursuant to the statement adopted by the Summit Meeting of the Security Council on 31 January 1992, 17 June 1992, UN Doc. A/47/277-S/24111.

55 Among these reviews see further United Nations, "Report of the High-level Independent Panel on Peace Operations on uniting our strengths for peace: politics, partnership and people", 16 June 2015, UN Doc. S/2015/446; United Nations, "The future of United Nations peace operations: implementation of the recommendations of the High-level Independent Panel on Peace Operations", 2 September 2015, UN Doc. S/2015/682; Radhika Coomaraswamy, "Preventing Conflict, Transforming Justice, Securing the Peace: A Global Study on the Implementation of United Nations Security Council resolution 1325", UN Women, 2015; United Nations, "Challenge of sustaining peace. Report of the Advisory Group of Experts on the Review of the Peacebuilding Architecture", 30 June 2015, UN Doc. S/2015/490.

56 United Nations, "Statement by the president of the Security Council", 20 February 2001, UN Doc. S/PRST/2001/5.

57 Based on United Nations, "Report of the Secretary-General on peacebuilding in the immediate aftermath of conflict", UN Doc. A/63/881-S/2009/304 (2009).

58 Kristian Berg Harpviken and Bernt A. Skåra, "Humanitarian mine action and peace building: Exploring the relationship", *Third World Quarterly*, Vol. 24, No. 5 (2003), p. 815.

59 UN Association in Canada, *Peacekeeping to Peacebuilding. Lessons from the Past. Building for the Future* (Ottawa, ON: UNAC, 2008), p. 93.

60 Juergen Dreding, "Human security and the UN Security Council", in Hideaki Shinoda and Ho-Won Jeong (eds), *Conflict and Human Security: A Search for New Approaches to Peace-building* (Hiroshima: Hiroshima University, 2004), pp. 87–88.

61 Fairlie Chappuis and Aditi Gorur, *Reconciling Security Sector Reform and the Protection of Civilians in Peacekeeping Contexts* (Washington, DC, and Geneva: Stimson/DCAF, 2014), pp. 4 and 6.

62 UN Security Council, "Update report: Security sector reform", 14 February 2007, www.securitycouncilreport.org/update-report/lookup-c-glKWLeMTIsG-b-2486441.php, p. 2; Albrecht Schnabel and Hans-Georg Ehrhart, "Post-conflict societies and the military: Challenges and problems of security sector reform", in Albrecht Schnabel and Hans-Georg Ehrhart (eds), *Security Sector Reform and Post-Conflict Peacebuilding* (Tokyo: United Nations University Press, 2005), p. 9.

63 Martin Barber, *Blinded by Humanity: Inside the UN's Humanitarian Operations* (London and New York: I. B. Tauris, 2015), p. 161.

64   United Nations, "Statement by the president of the Security Council", 19 November 2003, UN Doc. S/PRST/2003/22, p. 2.

65   Bob Kudyba and Andrea Poelling, "The military in peacekeeping operations", *Journal of Mine Action*, Vol. 8, No. 1 (2004), www.jmu.edu/cisr/journal/8.1/focus/kudyba/kudyba.htm.

66   Heiner Hänggi, "Approaching peacebuilding from a security governance perspective", in Alan Bryden and Heiner Hänggi (eds), *Security Governance in Post-Conflict Peacebuilding* (Münster: LIT, 2005), p. 13.

67   Harpviken and Skåra, note 58 above, p. 814.

68   Remarks by UN Deputy Secretary-General Jan Eliasson delivered at General Assembly debate on Integrating Crime Prevention and Criminal Justice in the Post-2015 Development Agenda, 25 February 2015.

69   Schnabel, note 4 above, p. 31.

70   Robert I. Rotberg, "Strengthening governance: Ranking countries would help", *Washington Quarterly*, Vol. 28, No. 1 (2004/2005), p. 71.

71   Michael Brzoska, "Security sector reform from a development donor perspective: Origins, theory and practice", in Heiner Hänggi and Theodor H. Winkler (eds), *Challenges of Security Sector Governance* (Münster: LIT, 2003), pp. 222 and 228–229.

72   Ibid., p. 220; Albrecht Schnabel and Vanessa Farr, "Returning to the development roots of security sector reform", in Albrecht Schnabel and Vanessa Farr (eds), *Back to the Roots: Security Sector Reform and Development* (Münster: LIT, 2012), p. 14; Schnabel, note 4 above, pp. 64–66.

73   Schnabel, ibid., p. 31.

74   Nao Shimoyachi-Yuzawa, "Linking demining to post-conflict peacebuilding: A case study of Cambodia", in David Jensen and Stephen Lonergan (eds), *Assessing and Restoring Natural Resources in Post-Conflict Peacebuilding* (London: Earthscan, 2012), p. 181.

75   Harpviken and Skåra, note 58 above, p. 815; UN General Assembly, "Resolution on assistance in mine action", 17 February 2004, UN Doc. A/RES/58/127; Harpviken and Isaksen, note 43 above; GICHD, note 43 above.

76   Introductory remarks by Helen Clark, UNDP administrator, at Peacebuilding Commission Retreat, Session 2: "Developing national capacity for peacebuilding", 25 March 2011, New York, quoted in UN Peacebuilding Support Office, *SSR and Peacebuilding. Thematic Review of Security Sector Reform (SSR) to Peacebuilding and the Role of the Peacebuilding Fund* (New York: United Nations, 2012), p. 55.

77   While in SSR the term "local ownership" is more regularly used, mine action refers to national ownership. However, both terms share the same fundamental principle that SSR processes and mine action activities must be designed, managed and implemented by domestic rather than external stakeholders. Ultimately, the beneficiaries of these activities should own the process.

78   Brzoska, note 71 above, p. 236; United Nations, "Securing peace and development: The role of the United Nations in supporting security sector reform", Report of the Secretary-General, 23 January 2008, UN Doc. A/62/659/2008/39, p. 13; United Nations, "Assistance in mine action", report of the Secretary-General, 9 August 2013, UN Doc. A/68/305; Kristian Berg Harpviken and Rebecca Roberts, "Conclusions", in Kristian Berg Harpviken and Rebecca Roberts (eds), *Preparing the Ground for Peace. Mine Action in Support of Peacebuilding* (Oslo: PRIO, 2004), p. 62.

79   UNMAS, "Guide for the application of International Mine Action Standards", 2003, IMAS 01.10, para 6.1, p. 3.

80   UN Security Council Resolution 2151 (2014), UN Doc. S/RES/2151 (2014), para. 2

81   Timothy Donais, "Operationalising local ownership", in Timothy Donais (ed.), *Local Ownership and Security Sector Reform* (Münster: LIT, 2008), pp. 276–277.

82   Alan Bryden, "Optimising mine action policies and practice", in Alan Bryden and Heiner Hänggi (eds), *Security Governance in Post-Conflict Peacebuilding* (Münster: LIT, 2005), p. 170; Alan Bryden, "Shaping the security governance agenda in post-conflict peacebuilding", in Alan Bryden and Heiner Hänggi (eds), *Security Governance in Post-Conflict Peacebuilding* (Münster: LIT, 2005), pp. 255 and 262.

83   Laurie Nathan, "The challenge of local ownership of SSR: From donor rhetoric to practice", in Timothy Donais (ed.), *Local Ownership and Security Sector Reform* (Münster: LIT, 2008), p. 21.

84   United Nations, "The strategy of the United Nations in mine action 2013–2018", www.mineaction.org/sites/default/files/publications/mine_action_strategy_mar15.pdf, p. 15.

85   GICHD, *A Guide on Transitioning Mine Action Programmes to National Ownership* (Geneva: GICHD, 2013), p. 7.

86   United Nations, "Report of the Secretary-General on peacebuilding in the immediate aftermath of conflict", 11 June 2009, UN Doc. A/63/881-S/2009/304.

87   Bryden, "Optimising mine action", note 82 above, p. 170.

88   Donais, note 81 above, p. 276.

89   See for instance François Bourguinon and Jean-Philippe Platteau, "The hard challenge of aid coordination", G-MonD Working Paper 33, Paris School of Economics, June 2013, pp. 1–2.

90   Hänggi, note 3 above, p. 11.

91   United Nations, note 6 above; Nicole Ball and Michael Brzoska with Kess Kingma and Herbert Wulf, "Voice and accountability in the security sector", report prepared for Human Development Report Office, BICC, Bonn, 2002, pp. 4 and 9.

92   Brzoska, note 71 above, p. 232.

93   Nicholas Galletti and Michael Wodzicki, "Securing human rights: Shifting the security sector reform paradigm", in Mark Sedra (ed.), *The Future of Security Sector Reform* (Waterloo, ON: CIGI, 2010), p. 289.

94   Hänggi, note 3 above, p. 18.

95   DCAF, "Security sector reform in post-conflict peacebuilding", DCAF Backgrounder, Geneva, 2009; Hänggi, note 66 above, p. 4.

96   Harpviken and Skåra, note 58 above, p. 816.

97   GICHD, *Guide to Strategic Planning in Mine Action* (Geneva: GICHD, 2014), pp. 23–24.

98   Harpviken and Roberts, note 78 above, p. 61; United Nations, note 6 above.

99   Interview with an international SSR expert, 31 August 2015.

100 Harpviken and Roberts, note 78 above, p. 62; Bryden, "Optimising mine action", note 82 above, pp. 173–174.

101 GICHD, note 33 above, p. 42.

102 Ibid., p. 43.

103 Ibid., pp. 45–46.

104 Bryden, "Optimising mine action", note 82 above, p. 173; Bryden, "Shaping the security governance agenda", note 82 above, p. 264.

105 For instance, APMBC, note 40 above, Art. 7; Convention on Cluster Munitions, CCM/77, 2008, Art. 7.

106 Sharp, note 22 above, pp. 172–173.

107 OECD-DAC, *SSR Handbook* (Paris: OECD, 2007), p. 21.

108 Sharp, note 22 above, pp. 172–174.

109 Galletti and Wodzicki, note 93 above, p. 286.

110 United Nations, "Human Rights Due Diligence Policy on United Nations Support to Non-United Nations Security Forces", 5 March 2013, UN Doc. A/67/775–S/2013/110.

111 United Nations, "Report of the special rapporteur on the promotion of truth, justice, reparation and guarantees of non-recurrence", 2012, UN Doc. A/HRC/21/46.

112 Sharp, note 22 above, pp. 174–175.

113 Galletti and Wodzicki, note 93 above, p. 281.

114 Sharp, note 22 above, pp. 175–176.

115 United Nations, "Human rights in Lebanon. Report of the special rapporteur on the right to food", 2006, UN Doc. A/HRC/2/8, p. 2.

116 United Nations, "Report of the independent expert on the situation of human rights in Somalia", 2012, UN Doc. A/HRC/21/61, p. 5.

117 Defined by UNMAS, note 31 above, as: "Persons either individually or collectively who have suffered physical, emotional and psychological injury, economic loss or substantial impairment of their fundamental rights through acts or omissions related to the use of mines or the presence of ERW. Victims include directly impacted individuals, their families, and communities affected by landmines and ERW."

118 Art. 6(3) of the APMBC, note 40 above, obliges each State Party in a position to do so to provide assistance for the care, rehabilitation and social and economic reintegration of mine victims.

119 Implementation Support Unit of the Anti-Personnel Mine Ban Convention, *Assisting Landmine and Other ERW Survivors in the Context of Disarmament, Disability and Development* (Geneva: ISU, 2011), p. 10.

120 Kerry Brinkert, "Understanding the Ottawa Convention's obligation to landmine victims", *Journal of Mine Action*, Vol. 10, No. 1 (2006).

121 Art. 8(2) of Protocol V to the CCW, note 38 above, provides for the care and rehabilitation and social and economic reintegration of victims of ERW. Arts 5 and 6 of the CCM, note 105 above, require States Parties to provide adequate age- and gender-sensitive assistance, including medical care, rehabilitation and psychological support, as well as provide for victims' social and economic inclusion, and assist other States Parties in doing so.

122 Implementation Support Unit of the Anti-Personal Mine Ban Convention, *Five Key Examples of the Role of Mine Action in Integrating Victim Assistance into Broader Frameworks* (Geneva: ISU, 2014), pp. 4–5.

123 Brinkert, note 120 above.

124 Maputo Action Plan 2014–2019, 27 June 2014, www.maputoreviewconference.org/fileadmin/APMBC-RC3/3RC-Maputo-action-plan-adopted-27Jun2014.pdf, Action 13.

125 United Nations, "Securing peace and development", note 78 above, p. 11.

126 OECD-DAC, "Section 9: Integrating gender awareness and equality", in *Handbook on Security Sector Reform* (Paris: OECD, 2011), p. 4.

127 Ibid., pp. 49, 66.

128 UN Security Sector Reform Unit, *The United Nations SSR Perspective* (New York: United Nations, 2012), p. 35.

129 CCM, note 105 above, Arts 5 and 6; Maputo Action Plan 2014–2019, note 124 above, Actions 10, 15 and 17.

130 Abigail Jones, Arianna Calza Bini and Stella Salvagni Varó, "How to improve demining activities through gender-sensitive mine risk education", *Journal of ERW and Mine Action*, Vol. 17, No. 1 (2013).

131 Galletti and Wodzicki, note 93 above, p. 288.

132 For this review we used the data in the UN mandate table, www.un.org/en/sc/repertoire/data.shtml#rel-1, 1 May 2015, and the missions' mandates. This table does not include UNSCO and MENUB. We also refer to special political missions as political/peacebuilding missions.

133 By "implicit" we mean that the linkage is "suggested though not directly expressed". Oxford Dictionary, www.oxforddictionaries.com.

134 This table summarizes information in Tables 2 and 3.

135 UN Security Council, Resolution 2227 (2015), para 14(b)(ii). The resolution stresses especially Part III and Annex 2 of the agreement, which are about the "reorganization of the armed and security forces", including profound SSR. See Agreement Chapter 10, www.derechos.org/peace/mali/doc/mali399.html.

136 UN Security Council, Resolution 2144 (1999), para. 10.

137 UN Security Council, Resolution 1244 (1999), para. 11(a), 11(c) and 11(f). Hänggi and Scherrer consider UNMIK as having a mandate in SSR even though it is not explicitly stated in the text. Heiner Hänggi and Vincenza Scherrer, "Recent experience of UN integrated missions in security sector reform", in Heiner Hänggi and Vincenza Scherrer (eds), *Security Sector Reform and UN Integrated Missions: Experience from Burundi, the Democratic Republic of Congo, and Kosovo* (Geneva: DCAF, 2007), pp. 14, 16 and 18.

138 The first priority is the protection of civilians and facilitation of humanitarian aid delivery; the third priority is the mediation of community conflicts, including addressing root causes. UN Security Council, Resolution 2228, 2015, UN Doc. S/RES/2228 (2015), para. 2.

139 Ibid., para. 8.

140 Doha Document for Peace in Darfur, Arts 56 and 74, al. 463, www.smallarmssurveysudan.org/fileadmin/docs/documents/Peace_Process_Chronology-DDPD.pdf.

141 This table is based on data in the UN mandate table, www.un.org/en/sc/repertoire/data.shtml#rel-1, 1 May 2015, and review of mandates. Explanations for single missions are in the text below the table or in endnotes.

142 UN Security Council, Resolution 1990 (2011), para. 2(c).

143 UN Security Council, Resolution 1996 (2011), para. 3(c)(vi).

144 UN Security Council, Resolution 1148 (1998), para. 1.

145 UN Security Council, Resolution 1701 (2006). It says that parties to the conflict should provide maps of landmines. UNIFIL conducts demining for operational reasons, but also for humanitarian reasons due to the situation in southern Lebanon. See www.unifil.missions.org/FAQS.

146 UN Security Council, note 135 above, para. 14(d)(iv).

147 UN Security Council, Resolution 2211 (2015), para 9(a).

148 See UNMAS website, "About UNMAS support of One UN and the GODRC", www.mineaction.org/programmes/drc.

149 UN Security Council, note 138 above, para. 2; United Nations, "Special report of the Secretary-General on the review of the African Union–United Nations Hybrid Operation in Darfur", 2014, UN Doc. S/2014/138, para. 40 and Annex I, p. 16.

150 UN Security Council, note 137 above, para. 9(e).

151 UN Security Council, Resolution 2149 (2014), UN Doc. S/RES/2149 (2014), para. 31(e).

152 Ibid., para. 33.

153 UN Security Council, Resolution 1509 (2003), para. 3(g).

154 UN Security Council, Resolution 2219 (2015), para. 21.

155 Ibid., para. 23.

156 Ibid., para. 11.

157 See UNMAS website, "UNMAS mandate, in support of UNOCI", www.mineaction.org/programmes/civ.

158 SSR is identified explicitly as part of the third tier of DPKO's 2015 policy on Protection of Civilians. Policy on the Protection of Civilians in United Nations Peacekeeping (New York: UN Department of Peacekeeping Operations and Department of Field Support, 2015).

159 This table is based on data in the UN mandate table, www.un.org/en/sc/repertoire/data.shtml#rel-1, 1 May 2015, and explanations for single missions are in the text below the table or in endnotes.

160 UN Security Council, Resolution 2210 (2015), para. 7. UNAMA is called upon to ensure the "ONE UN" approach among UN agencies, funds and programmes.

161 UNAMI shall "promote the protection of human rights and judicial and legal reform in order to strengthen the rule of law in Iraq". UN Security Council, Resolution 1770 (2007), para. 2(c).

162 United Nations, "Report of the Secretary-General on the United Nations Support Mission in Libya", 2015, UN Doc. S/2015/144, paras 64 and 66.

163 UN Security Council, Resolution 2232 (2015), UN Doc. S/RES/2232 (2015), p. 2.

164 UN Security Council, note 161 above, para. 4.

165 Ibid., paras 6(e), 7, 7(c) and 30. See also p. 6. UNMAS assists the Afghan National Disaster Management Authority to address the issue of landmines and ERW. See Mine Action, "Afgahnistan", www.mineaction.org/programmes/afghanistan.

166 UN Security Council, Resolution 2158 (2014), para. 1(b)(ii) and 1(c)(i); see also UN Security Council, note 163 above, para. 21.

167 UN Security Council, Resolution 2213 (2015), para. 9(c). UNSMIL has stopped its direct support to some components of SSR due to the instability in Libya, but continues to promote them in the current political dialogue with local stakeholders.

168 United Nations, note 162 above, paras 64 and 66.

169 Ibid., para. 65.

170 UN Security Council, note 167 above, para. 9(b).

171 UN Security Council, note 137 above, para. 6(c).

172 The need for stronger linkage is also proven by the fact that SSR is "heavily dependent" on related activities like DDR, SALW control, mine action and transitional justice. Hänggi, note 16 above, p. 30.

173 United Nations, note 6 above, para. 17.

174 Ibid., paras 55 and 61(d).

175 Ibid., paras 56 and 61(g). The importance of "recognizing the interlinkages between security sector reform and other important factors of stabilization and reconstruction", is also stressed by UN Security Council Resolution 2151. UN Security Council, note 80, above, p. 2.

176 See Figure 1 in this paper.

177 This issue is highlighted by UN Security Council Resolution 2151: "the failure to address operational and accountability deficits can undermine the positive gains of peacekeeping and necessitates the return of peacekeeping and special political missions in previous areas of operation". UN Security Council, note 80 above, p. 2.

178 The Maputo Action Plan was adopted on 27 June 2014 during the last APMBC review conference, and reaffirms States Parties' commitment to mine action and to implement the plan in a "cooperative, inclusive, age-appropriate and gender-sensitive manner".

179 CCM, note 105 above, Art. 5.

180 Kjell Erling Kjellman and Kristian Berg Harpviken, "Meeting the challenge. National ownership in mine action", PRIO Policy Brief 1/2006 Assistance to Mine-Affected Communities, Oslo, 2006; UNMAS, note 79 above, IMAS 01.10, para 6.1, p. 3.

181 "Completion" in mine action refers to fulfilling APMBC Art. 5 and CCM Art. 3 for countries that have signed these conventions, and fulfilling country-specific completion targets for countries that are not signatories to these conventions.

182 Residual contamination in this context refers to the mine/ERW contamination that is discovered after all reasonable effort has been made to identify and process all suspected areas. In the context of key conventions such as the APMBC and CCM, residual contamination refers to the anti-personnel landmines and cluster munitions that are discovered after clearance obligations have been fulfilled and the country has declared "completion" of respective articles.

183 EOD is defined as: "the detection, identification, evaluation, render safe, recovery and disposal of explosive ordnance (EO)". EOD may be undertaken: "a) as a routine part of mine clearance operations, upon discovery of ERW; b) to dispose of ERW discovered outside hazardous areas, (this may be a single item of ERW, or a larger number inside a specific area); or c) to dispose of EO which has become hazardous by deterioration, damage or attempted destruction". UNMAS, note 31 above, IMAS 04.10, para 3.97, p. 14.

184 GICHD, *National Capacities and Residual Contamination: Liberia* (Geneva: GICHD, 2014), p. 12.

185 Ibid., pp. 14–15.

186 Ibid., p. 17.

187 Lee Moroney and Kay Gamst, "Self-Help Ammunition Destruction Options Worldwide (SHADOW)", *Journal of ERW and Mine Action*, Vol. 17, No. 3 (2013); NPA, *Self-Help Options for Destruction of Cluster Munition Stockpiles* (Oslo: NPA 2010), pp. 13–14.

188 NPA, ibid., p. 13.

189 Interview with an NPA representative, September 2014.

190 Ibid.

191 Ted Paterson, Prabin Chitrakar and Abigail Hartley, *Evaluation of the UN Mine Action in Nepal* (Geneva: GICHD, 2012).

192 Ibid., p. 36.

193 Ibid., pp. 29, 36.

194 IMSMA is a software program developed by the GICHD in the late 1990s; its goal is to provide a comprehensive information package for mine action. See GICHD, "Information management/ IMSMA", www.gichd.org/mine-action-topics/management-of-mine-action-programmes/information-management-imsma/#.VjDteNJVhBc.

195 Informal Sector Service is a Nepal human rights NGO created in 1988. Paterson et al., note 191 above, pp. 9–12. See also the NGO's website, www.insec.org.np.

196 Paterson et al., ibid., pp. 36, 38.

197 The Comprehensive Peace Accord signed by the government of Nepal and the Communist Party of Nepal (Maoist) encompassed a number of policies aiming to transform the country's institutional setting and socio-economic system. The accord included a chapter on management of armies and arms, designed to support the elections of the Constituent Assembly and the process of democratizing and restructuring the army. United Nations, "Special political missions", report of the Secretary-General, 2013, p. 9.

198 The situation in Ukraine is not fully post-conflict, but the need for mine action institutions was present before the current crisis due to issues related to the destruction of stockpiles of mines and contamination from past conflicts. In addition, as shown in Figure 3, post-conflict peacebuilding is not limited by the establishment of a ceasefire, but can take place even before peacekeeping and overlap with peacemaking and peace enforcement. Finally, it is worth mentioning that at the time of writing, according to the International Crisis Group the "ceasefire in the east has largely held since 1 September". International Crisis Group, "Russia and separatists in eastern Ukraine", Crisis Group Europe and Central Asia Briefing No. 79, February 2016, p. 1.

199 The SES was put under the Ministry of Interior in April 2014. *Gazeta Liv*, 25 April 2014, www.gazeta.lviv.ua/news/2014/04/25/28088.

200 A conference in April 2015, organized jointly by the OSCE PCU, DCAF and the GICHD, showed that stakeholders in Ukraine are aware of the challenges of coordinating mine action among different state institutions.

201 Presidential Decree 423 on "Mine Action National Authority", 2 September 2014. See Norwegian People's Aid, *Clearing the Mines: Report for the Fourteenth Meeting of States Parties to the Anti-Personnel Mine Ban Convention* (Oslo: NPA, 2015), p. 201.

202 See European Union Advisory Mission, "The mandate", www.euam-ukraine.eu/en/about_euam/the_mandate. See also Council of the EU, press release, 22 July 2014, www.consilium.europa.eu/uedocs/cms_Data/docs/pressdata/EN/foraff/144079.pdf.

203 Protection Cluster Ukraine, "The protection cluster includes sub-clusters on child protection, gender based violence and mine action", June 2015, http://reliefweb.int/sites/reliefweb.int/files/resources/gpc_factsheet_june_2015_en_0.pdf.

204 Danish Refugee Council, "Ukraine", http://drc.dk/relief-work/where-we-work/ukraine/.

205 Fondation Suisse de Déminage, "FSD Offices", http://fsd.ch/about-fsd/fsd-offices; ITF Enhancing Human Security, "Enhancing psychosocial wellbeing of children from Ukraine", www.itf-fund.si/about-us/itf-and-slovenias-development-cooperation#enhancing-psychosocial-wellbeing-of-children-from-ukraine.

206 OSCE PCU, "OSCE Project Coordinator in Ukraine: Mandate", www.osce.org/ukraine/106005.

207 Ibid.

208 NATO, "NATO Trust Fund Projects", www.nspa.nato.int/en/organization/logistics/LogServ/ntfp.htm.

209 Danish Relief Council, "Protection cluster factsheet", July 2015, http://drc.dk/relief-work/where-we-work/ukraine/.

210 GICHD, "OSCE signs memorandum of understanding with the GIHCD and DCAF to consolidate humanitarian action in Ukraine", 25 September 2015, www.gichd.org/what-we-do/gichd-news/news-detail/article/1443194693-osce-signs-a-memorandum-of-understanding-with-the-gichd-and-dcaf-to-consolidate-humanitarian-action-in-ukraine/#.VjiJQdJVhBc; International Geneva, "Conference on Ukraine security, humanitarian demining and explosive remnants of war challenges organized by GICHD, DCAF and OSCE, Maison de la Paix, 28–29 April 2015", www.geneve-int.ch/conference-ukraine-s-current-security-humanitarian-demining-and-explosive-remnants-war-erw-challenge.

211 Boubacar N'Diaye, "Security sector reform in the Central African Republic", in Hans Born and Albrecht Schnabel (eds), *Security Sector Reform in Challenging Environments* (Münster: LIT, 2009), pp. 41–43, 56 and 61; Teodora Fuior and David Law, "Security sector reform in the Central African Republic. Chronicle of a death foretold", SSR 2.0 Brief No. 1, October 2014, p. 1.

212 Secretary-General's remarks to a group of journalists at UN Headquarters, New York, 11 February 2014, www.un.org/sg/offthecuff/index.asp?nid=3304.

213 United Nations, "Report of the Secretary-General on the Central African Republic submitted pursuant to paragraph 48 of Security Council Resolution 2127 (2013)", 3 March 2014, UN Doc. S/2014/142; United Nations, "Letter from the Secretary-General addressed to the President of the Security Council", 16 September 2013, UN Doc. S/2013/557; Amnesty International, *Central African Republic. Human Rights Crisis Spiralling Out of Control* (London: Amnesty International, 2013), pp. 5–6; DCAF/ISSAT, "Background note: Central African Republic", February 2, 2015, http://issat.dcaf.ch/Learn/Resource-Library/Country-Profiles/Central-African-Republic-Background-Note#11.

214 United Nations, "Secretary-General's remarks to the Security Council on the situation in the Central African Republic", New York, 20 February 2014, www.un.org/sg/statements/index.asp?nid=7471.

215 UN Security Council, note 80 above.

216 UN Security Council, note 151 above.

217 United Nations, "Report of the Secretary-General", note 213 above.

218 UN Security Council, note 151 above.

219 United Nations, "Report of the Secretary-General", note 213 above.

220 Mine Action, "About UNMAS in Central African Republic", www.mineaction.org/programmes/centralafricanrepublic.

221 United Nations, "USG Hervé Ladsous inaugurates construction of the Kassaï central armoury", press release, 12 May 2015, www.mineaction.org/news/usg-herv%C3%A9-ladsous-inaugurates-construction-kassai-central-armoury.

222 UNMAS, "Statement by Richard Derieux, UNMAS programme director, MINUSCA, at the opening of the construction of the central armoury Camp Kassaï", 27 April 2015, www.mineaction.org/sites/default/files/documents/UNMAS_Derieux_Camp%20Kassai_27042015.pdf; United Nations, "Report of the Secretary-General on the situation in the Central African Republic", 29 July 2015, UN Doc. S/2015/576.

223 UN Security Council, note 151 above.

224 UN Security Council, note 80 above.

225 United Nations, "Statement by the Secretary-General of the United Nations at the 7161st meeting of the Security Council on maintenance of international peace and security", 28 April 2014, UN Doc. S/PV.7161.

226 Hervé Ladsous stated: "mes équipes m'ont également fait part des initiatives du Ministère de la défense et de son état-major avec le soutien des forces internationales de procéder à la vérification de ses éléments avant leur retour opérationnel, faisant montre de votre volonté de vous doter d'une armée irréprochable et répondant progressivement aux normes internationales". United Nations, "USG Hervé Ladsous inaugurates construction of the Kassaï central armoury", press release, 12 May 2015, http://mineaction.org/news/usg-herv%C3%A9-ladsous-inaugurates-construction-kassai-central-armoury.

227 Naidoo, note 45 above, pp. 1–8.

228 Denise Garcia, *Disarmament Diplomacy and Human Security: Regimes, Norms and Moral Progress in International Relations* (London and New York: Routledge, 2011).

229 Stefano Migliorisi and Anwesha Phabhr, *Guatemala: World Bank Country-Level Engagement on Governance and Anti-Corruption* (Washington, DC: World Bank Group, 2011), p. 1.

230 International Crisis Group, "Corridor of violence: The Guatemala–Honduras border", *Latin America Report*, No. 52, 4 June 2014, p. 2.

231 International Crisis Group, "Policy reform in Guatemala: Obstacles and opportunities", *Latin America Report*, No. 43, 20 July 2012, pp. 4–5.

232 GICHD, *Mine Action and Armed Violence Reduction. OAS SALW and Munitions Destruction Programme. Guatemala Case Study* (Geneva: GICHD, 2012), pp. 4–5.

233 Ibid., p. 4.

234 Ibid., p. 10.

235 United Nations, "Small arms and light weapons", report of the Secretary-General, 27 April 2015, UN Doc. S/2015/289.

236 GICHD, note 232 above, pp. 11–12.

237 Ibid., p. 13.

238 Ibid., p. 20.

239 OCHA, "Joint factsheet on Karamoja: Humanitarian and development realities in the region", OCHA, Kampala, 2008, p. 1.

240 James Bevan, *Crisis in Karamoja – Armed Violence and the Failure of Disarmament in Uganda's Most Deprived Region* (Geneva: Small Arms Survey, 2008), p. 42.

241 Saferworld, *Karamoja Conflict and Security Assessment* (London: Saferworld, 2010).

242 Kees Kingma, Frank Muhereza, Ryan Murray, Matthias Nowak and Lilu Thapa, *Security Provision and Small Arms in Karamoja. A Survey of Perceptions* (Geneva: SAS/DDG, 2012), p. 16.

243 DDG, *DDG's Armed Violence Reduction Framework* (Copenhagen: DDG, 2012).

244 GICHD, *Mine Action and Armed Violence Reduction. Danish Demining Group Community Safety Programme. Uganda Case Study* (Geneva: GICHD, 2012), pp. 7–9.

245 Ibid., pp. 9–10.

246 Ibid., p. 11.

247 Ibid., p. 12.

248 Ibid.

249 Savannah de Tessières, *Enquête nationale sur les armes légères et de petit calibre en Côte d'Ivoire. Les défis du contrôle des armes et de la lutte contre la violence armée avant la crise postélectorale* (Geneva: Small Arms Survey, 2012).

250 GICHD, *Mine Action and Armed Violence Reduction. UNMAS Physical Security and Stockpile Management Pilot Programme. Côte d'Ivoire Case Study* (Geneva: GICHD, 2012), p. 5.

251 UN Security Council, Resolution 2000 (2011), UN Doc. S/RES/2000 (2011).

252 Since late 2012 UNMAS has reported to the deputy special representative of the Secretary-General.

253 Interview with an international mine action expert, 11 August 2015.

254 GICHD, note 250 above, p. 9.

255 UNOCI, "Réforme du secteur de la sécurité" ("Security sector reform"), *La Force de la paix. Bulletin thématique*, Vol. 4, No. 1 (2013), p. 7.

256 GICHD, note 250 above, pp. 6–10; United Nations, "Assistance in mine action", note 78 above; HALO Trust, "Where we work", www.halotrust.org/where-we-work.

257 United Nations, ibid.

258 UNOCI, note 255 above.

259 GICHD, note 250 above, pp. 17–18.

260 MAG, "Burundi", www.maginternational.org/mag/en/where-mag-works/burundi/#.VipTzdKqqko.

261 GICHD, *Mine Action and Armed Violence Reduction. Mines Advisory Group's Physical Security and Stockpile Management Programme. Burundi Case Study* (Geneva: GICHD, 2012), p. 19.

262 Focused on behavioural change within the security and justice sectors, the programme provides targeted training in management and strategic planning in addition to training in ethics and human rights. See CIGI, "Burundi No. 4", *Security Sector Monitor*, October 2010.

263 Nicole Ball, *Putting Governance at the Heart of Security Sector Reform. Lessons from the Burundi– Netherlands Security Sector Development Programme* (The Hague: Clingendael, 2014), pp. 15, 44.

264 GICHD, note 261 above, p. 19.

265 John Blaney, Jacques Paul Klein and Sean McFate, "Wider lessons for peacebuilding: Security sector reform in Liberia", Policy Analysis Brief, Stanley Foundation, June 2010, p. 7; Mark Sedra, "Afghanistan", in Alan Bryden and Vincenza Scherrer (eds), *Disarmament, Demobilization and Reintegration and Security Sector Reform. Insights from UN Experience in Afghanistan, Burundi, the Central African Republic and the Democratic Republic of Congo* (Münster: LIT, 2012), p. 42.

266 United Nations, "Integrated DDR standards. 06.10: DDR and security sector reform", 2009, p. 5, www.iddrtg.org/wp-content/uploads/2013/05/IDDRS-6.10-DDR-SSR1.pdf.

267 Candace Karp and Richard Ponzio, "NATO, SSR and Afghanistan", in David Law (ed.), *International Organisations and Security Sector Reform* (Münster: LIT, 2007), p. 220.

268 GICHD, *Mine Action and Armed Violence Reduction. HALO Trust's Reintegration of Former Combatants Into Demining. Afghanistan Case Study* (Geneva: GICHD, 2012), pp. 5–6. See also Arne Strand, "Transforming local relationships: Reintegration of combatants through mine action In Afghanistan", in Kristian Berg Harpviken and Rebecca Roberts (eds), *Preparing the Ground for Peace. Mine Action in Support of Peacebuilding* (Oslo: PRIO, 2004), pp. 39–54.

269 Steven A. Zyck, *Peace and Reintegration: An Introduction. Part 1 of a Four-Part Series on Peace and Reintegration in Afghanistan* (Norfolk, VA: NATO Civil–Military Fusion Center, 2012), pp. 4–7.

270 GICHD, note 268 above, pp. 7–12.

271 Ibid., pp. 12, 15.

272 In addition to improved community relations, HALO Trust recognizes the potential for attracting funding for activities that can serve both demining and DDR objectives. As many donors are currently cutting back on spending, dual-purpose activities provide extra value for money. Ibid., p. 7.

273 Ibid., p. 16.

274 Georg Frerks, Geert Gompelman and Stefan van Laar with Bart Klem, *The Struggle after Combat. The Role of NGOs in DDR Processes: Afghanistan Case Study* (The Hague: Cordaid, 2008), p. 21.

275 Blaney et al., note 265 above, p. 1.

276 GICHD, note 268 above, p. 16; Frerks et al., note 274 above, p. 21.

277 Zyck, note 269 above, p. 8; Mark Checchia, *Security Aspects of Peace and Reintegration. Part 4 of a Four-Part Series on Peace and Reintegration in Afghanistan* (Norfolk, VA: NATO Civil–Military Fusion Center, 2012), pp. 3–4.

278 United Nations, note 6 above, ch. IV.